erybody who's doing it all that happy?How far is really to
ver feel like used goods? If you wear a condom, you'r
right? What if that pregnancy test turns blue? Can you ge
from oral sex? Waiting for Mr. or Ms. Right? How are yo
osed to know? Is everybody who's doing it all that happy
far is really too far? Ever feel like used goods?If you wea
dom, you're safe, right? What if that pregnancy test turn
Can you get STDs from oral sex? Waiting for Mr. or M
? How are you supposed to know? Is everybody who
it all that happy? How far is really too far? Ever feel lik
goods?If you wear a condom, you're safe, right? What

Want somebody to love you for you?

Then it's time to Come Clean.

You deserve respect.

You deserve the info.

You deserve to make your own choices.

Right now.

come clean

it's about sex • it's about your future • it's about what you deserve

come

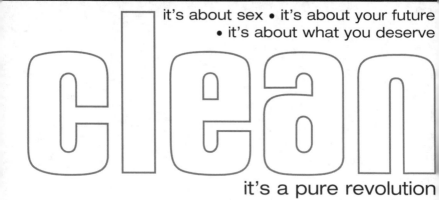

it's about sex • it's about your future • it's about what you deserve

clean

it's a pure revolution

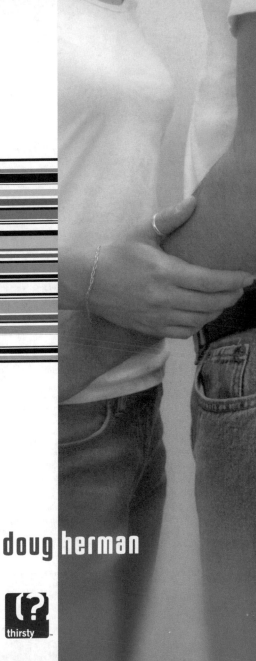

doug herman

Tyndale House Publishers
Wheaton, Illinois

Visit Tyndale's thirsty(?) Web site at areUthirsty.com and Doug Herman at PureRevolution.com

Published in association with the literary agency of The B & B Media Group, Inc., dba The Barnabas Agency, 109 S. Main, Corsicana, TX 75110.

Designed by Jacqueline Noe

Library of Congress Cataloging-in-Publication Data

Herman, Doug, date.
  Come clean : fight the sexual battle, protect your future, demand what you deserve / Doug Herman.
      p. cm.
Includes bibliographical references.
    ISBN 0-8423-8358-1 (pbk.)
    1. Chastity. 2. Christian teenagers—Sexual behavior. 3. Sexual abstinence—Religious aspects—Christianity. 4. Sex instruction for teenagers—Religious aspects—Christianity.
I. Title.
BV4647.C5H465 2004
241'.66—dc22   2003023678

Printed in the United States of America

10   09   08   07   06   05   04
 7   6   5   4   3   2   1

To the thousands of teens whose faces I see in schools and youth conferences every month . . . you are the reason I keep fighting. May your future be forever changed.

To Josh, Bri, and Luc, my three children. I pray this book becomes the beginning of a new movement of coming clean that touches each of your lives personally. May it impact the lives of your future in-laws, so that they raise your future spouse with courage, wisdom, and purity. May it empower you as you become adults. May it afford you a marriage that is pure and fulfilling . . . and bring to all of us the contagious laughter of yet unborn grandchildren.

> I have fought a good fight,
> I have finished the race,
> and I have remained faithful.
> —2 Timothy 4:7

contents

Most of us probably didn't ever dream of making a career talking about sex.

But that's exactly what I do. And I love it.

So how did I get here, and why would you care what I have to say?

It's simple. I think teens are the most exciting people to be around. You have a strength unlike any generation before yours. I love standing in schools and watching 1,000 faces as I'm introduced as a speaker who talks about relationships and abstinence.

And I love watching those same faces as I share about my daughter Ashli.

You see, AIDS killed my little girl.

She was only two years old when she died. As I stood beside her frail body, I had a tough decision to make. A breathing machine was the only thing keeping her alive—she was one flip of a switch away from death. The doctor told me, "Her lungs are now filled with fluid. We can possibly extend her life for two more days, with medication, but . . . " His voice trailed off. Then he continued, "If you shut the machines off today, she'll die in a couple of hours. If you don't, she'll suffer for two days and then die. What do you want to do, Doug? It's your choice."

My choice.

My daughter was dying. *That* was not my choice.

And there was absolutely nothing I could do about it. That was not my choice either.

Ashli was born with AIDS. My wife, Evon, had gotten it from a blood transfusion and passed it on to our baby. And I had to choose the date and the time for my daughter to die.

There was no miracle or solution for Ashli. So I leaned over and kissed her. "Sweetheart, I'm sorry about the pain. I'm sorry about the hurt, the suffering, and your short life. But I am *not* sorry you are my little girl. I'm not sorry we had two years and two months together. I'm not sorry that I love you. And I'm not sorry that I get to see you again in heaven someday. I love you, Ashli. Good-bye." There could never be enough words or enough time to say all the things I wanted to say to her. Never enough time to hold her and feel her warm breath on my face.

I called the nurse in, and she shut off the machine. Ashli took two breaths and died.*

Eight months after AIDS killed my little girl, it killed my wife. Half my family. As I sat by my daughter's deathbed, and later my wife's, I hated that disease more than I had ever hated anything.

Evon and I never chose HIV—we just wanted to have a family. I had never made a choice to be involved in high-risk sexual activity and then lie about my past on a blood donor form. Only the donor, whose blood infected Evon and Ashli, had chosen that. And with his choice, he had stripped away two precious lives and my family's dreams.

Think I was angry? Oh yeah. But the two death certificates I held in my hand gave me a passion: There was no way I'd sit by and let the same thing happen to anyone else. Not to you. And not to your friends. It's personal to me.

So that's why I stand in gymnasiums across the country talking about sex.

Come Clean is a blunt look at sex and relationships. It's about more passion than you've ever imagined. And students like you all over the country are discovering it.

Come Clean is all about you. Your life, your hopes, your dreams.

It's about sex. It's about your future. It's about what you deserve.

Doug Herman

---

* Adapted from the story told in Doug Herman, *FaithQuake: Rebuilding Your Faith After Tragedy Strikes* (Grand Rapids, Mich.: Baker Books, 2003), 21.

Sex.

Okay, so we've got the topic. And I'm guessing you've got the interest. Most of us do. After all, we're wired to want it. And nothing on earth is quite like it. But we'll get to that soon enough.

First let's imagine . . .

Imagine you saw an ad that said: "Don't drink and drive . . . but if you do, or if you ride in a car with a drunk driver, be sure to buckle up!" That would be ridiculous, wouldn't it?

Or what if another ad said, "Smoking cigarettes causes lung cancer and shortens your life. But if you can't stop, use filters to smoke safely"?

Or what if, when your friends are binge drinking, someone told them, "You really should cut consumption . . . in half"? No, the fact is, binge drinking can kill.

Or what if a sign over your school's entrance said, "Violence is your right . . . so if you feel you must fight—fight carefully"? Or, "If you're going to carry a gun to school, come see the office about how to fire it in the safest way"? No, instead we have metal detectors to keep weapons *out* of students' hands.

In all these cases *risk elimination* is the best approach. We work hard to remove any chance of those we care about getting hurt. Why then do we settle only for *risk reduction* when it comes to sex outside of marriage, especially when so much is at stake?

If you care about your friends, you don't want them to get hurt. And that includes challenging them to avoid high-risk behavior, because it can hurt or even kill them or someone else.

You have a choice. Blood systems are safer than they've ever been. The only way you'd get AIDS, or any sexually-transmitted infection, unplanned pregnancy, emotional pain, or skewed future plans resulting from high-risk sexual activity is if you *choose* to be involved in it.

So you must make a choice.

What do you want your life to be like down the road? As you read the stories in the following pages, realize that it's never too early to start thinking about what you deserve.

You deserve respect.

You deserve to make your own choices.

You deserve a great future and a family.

You deserve laughter, not tears.

You deserve real love and lifelong relationships.

Do you care about yourself? Do you really care about your friends?

What will you choose?

bombarded by it

Sex Affects . . . and the Effects of Sex

Picture this.

You're driving down the highway, talking on your cell, flipping the radio station, and scratching your nose, when you glance up at the road and your eyes meet . . . skin. A billboard with an ad for suntan oil that's advertising something besides oil.

Or maybe you're doing your algebra homework in front of the TV on any given night, when your attention is distracted from $x + y = z$ by that couple who *finally* got together and are now rolling around on top of the sheets. So much for algebra.

Or maybe the guy or girl you're dating is heading toward third base (sexually speaking) but you're not sure you're ready to leave the batter's box. Do you step up to the plate and bunt so at least you don't strike out?

There's a whole lotta sex out there, and it seems people everywhere are doing it.

Have you ever spent time thinking about what you believe when it comes to sex? You know, things like how far you'd go on a first date and whether it bothers you that most TV shows keep pushing the limits: he slept with her who slept with his roommate last night but not the night before because he was with her best friend but she'd like to get something going with his brother who's already thinking the same thing. Do they ever get any *sleep*?

Don't get me wrong. Sex is amazing. It would have to be to have the moneymaking power and influence that it has in our world.

But does this idea of right and wrong have anything to do with it? Is there harm in enjoying several partners, playing the field to satisfy the natural sex drive that's just part of being human?

Bluntly, yes. There is.

If you feel like tossing this book across the room, please read some more.

The Ripple Effect

Remember good old Isaac Newton and the law of gravity he discovered when an apple fell on his head? Well, his third law of motion states that "for every action, there is an equal and opposite reaction." Isaac was a smart guy. Every choice we make *does* create a reaction or consequence. It's crazy to think we can do something and have zero consequences. Just like throwing a rock into a pond creates a ripple effect, so does every choice you make—including whether or not to have sex when you're single.

Did you get that? Where'd that standard come from, and who says it's right?

Actually, I wasn't the one who came up with the idea that sex belongs only in marriage. That standard comes straight from the top—from God himself. We'll talk about that in the next chapter.

For now, let's agree on a definition.

What is sex?

You may be thinking, *Wow, this guy's really getting back to basics.* Well, I'd just like to clear up something.

Some people believe that having sex means only sexual intercourse. Your peers might not consider oral and anal sex, fondling, or mutual masturbation to be sex. But here's the truth: High-risk sexual activity for two unmarried people is ANY genital contact of any kind. Even with a condom, any genital activity is a risk. (To find out more on why, see chapters 6 and 7.) And with any risky action, there will be an equal and opposite reaction.

Let's get it straight, right off the bat.

Sex does not equal love. But people have fallen for that lie for—well, forever. And generations have dealt with the consequences—unnecessary pain, guilt, and regret, as well as diseases, unplanned pregnancies, missed dreams, and family meltdowns.

It may seem hard to believe that sex can lead to all those consequences. After all, how can something that's supposed to be so fun be bad?

I'm not saying sex is bad. Not by a long shot. Take a look at the picture on the cover. Those people are actually a married couple. See, it's not that God forbids us to hold someone close and intimate like that. The point is that sex outside of marriage never brings good results.

> **High-risk sexual activity for two unmarried people is ANY genital contact of ANY kind.**

I'd like to introduce to you a young woman I'll call Kari. She wrote me this letter after I spoke in her school in Nebraska. As you read it, maybe you'll recognize part of a friend's story—or maybe your own.

> *When I was 11, I started middle school. Around homecoming, I started seeing this high school senior who was nice to me. We spent almost every day together for two months, then broke up because he was going off to college. We only had sex once, but I live with the guilt every day. I had promised myself I wasn't going to do that until I found someone worth it.*

So for over a year I didn't have sex with anyone. I was so proud of myself. Then an old boyfriend came back into my life.

He said just being around me made him want to be better. I told him right away that I did have feelings for him but if anything happened, we would take it SLOW. Well, things went great for a while, but then we had sex. I think I did it for fear of losing someone who actually liked me. I've promised myself to "stay single." But once you've had sex, it's just so hard.

Doug, I'll never forget what you said: "If you've done an adult activity—had sex—then do another adult activity: get tested for STDs. It's called responsibility." I was scared—what would my parents say?

You said that you were here for the people in the room who have had sex already, and that we can start over. Thank you for not thinking of nonvirgin teens as losers. Right then and there I decided I could do it—make a choice to not have sex and stick to it.

Then I went home and took a shower. I found a bump "down there." I didn't know what to think . . . could it be an ingrown hair from shaving—or something else? My last boyfriend had been around. And while we did use a condom, I know they're not foolproof. Well, I just started to cry. My mind jumped to the worst possibilities.

I really needed to talk to someone. I knew my friends wouldn't understand and would gossip about me. My brother would think I was joking. My dad would kill me. So I decided my mom was the best choice—even though I hate disappointing her.

So I asked her, no matter what, not to hate me. I came clean with her—and it felt good. We discussed things we've never talked about before. She didn't yell or run off. She actually sat there and talked to me.

And together we made the doctor appointment. I'm going tomorrow. I'm really scared, but my mom is going with me.

Kari's world has been rocked. Sex wasn't glue that held her relationship together. It didn't keep her boyfriend from leaving her to go to college. It didn't create commitment or undying love.

Instead, sex with a guy she wasn't married to left Kari dealing with guilt every time she opens her eyes in the morning. Not only that, Kari has to worry about disappointing her parents and getting sexually transmitted diseases.

But what about romance and affection?

Everybody needs some of that in a relationship, right? But here's the catch—true romance isn't selfish. True romance is about the other person. If the only reason your date holds your hand or rubs your back is because he's hoping to score later, he is being selfish. Romance isn't the same thing as sex. It isn't something you do in order to get sex. It's about sharing each other's heart and soul.

> Romance isn't something you do to get sex.

The Soul

The soul is the deepest part of a person—the part that makes you *you.* Your identity, your hopes and dreams, your spirituality—the deep-down *life* inside you. It's the part of yourself that you wish people knew, but at the same time you'd be terrified if anyone knew all that's there. Your soul has both emotional and spiritual needs. And if those needs of love and acceptance, of being really known and understood, aren't met, your soul hurts.

In order to have a great dating relationship, both the guy and girl need to have those soul-needs met.

So how does sex before marriage get in the way of that? Look at it this way. Imagine these two balloons are the inner hearts or souls of two people.

When you first meet someone, that very brief encounter makes him or her an acquaintance. Nothing deep or permanent connects you. It's as if a small piece of thread wraps around two balloons. If one of you were to leave forever, the thread would be easily broken. And the loss wouldn't be that great.

But the more the two of you get to know each other, the more

pieces of thread begin to tie you together. As your relationship progresses, the thread becomes string.

Each experience with that person is represented by another piece of string. The more time you spend together, the more string bonds your hearts together. And the more shared experiences, the more painful the loss or separation will be. It's like the difference between just anyone in your school moving to another state and your best

friend moving to another state. The memories you have together will last a lifetime, even if you're not always together.

If your friend is the opposite sex and the two of you decide to step things up to a romantic level, the bond intensifies. Those strings are now a cable. And this cable begins to bind you all the more tightly.

All Chained Up?

Now let's say you add sex to the relationship. Because the two of you reveal the most private areas of your bodies, allow the other person to

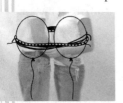

touch you there, and then share intercourse, a soul connection occurs. Stronger than a cable, sex is like a chain that fastens two lives in an unforgettable moment that can never be taken back.

At this point, without question, the two of you are bound together. God designed this chain bonding for marriage—a loving, committed relationship. Two people become one, soul-to-soul, body-to-body, for life. But the pain is unbelievable when there's no marriage bond. Breakups

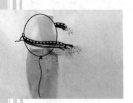

hurt even more when sex has been a part of the relationship. Some of you know what I mean. Your heart is wrenched in two.

Each string, cable, and chain wrapped around your heart represents a memory of a shared experience. Those ties can never be removed from your soul. They make up the deepest part of you. Many people try to heal from a breakup by jumping into another relationship. That merely compounds the pain.

> Each sexual experience creates an intimate bond whether you want it to or not. There's no way around it.

TV and movies tend to show only the fun side of sex. But in real life it's impossible to hop into bed for all of the fun and none of the consequences. Each sexual experience creates an intimate bond whether you want it to or not. There's no way around it. Sex affects you deep inside, and its effects are long lasting. It was designed that way. But experiencing sex doesn't mean you've experienced love.

That's what the next chapter is all about.

2

a perfect plan
The Way God Made It

Love is a verb.

Over the decades, writers and musicians have written zillions of songs about love. Some have messed-up ideas of what love really is, claiming it's all about feelings. Others say that love is about sex. But God's kind of love is a verb, requiring action to show its power and depth. Your actions prove whether you really love someone.

And that doesn't mean using someone to get what you want. Loving someone means looking out for that person's best interests rather than your urges. True love isn't just a feeling, because feelings come and go. True love is based on long-term, lifetime commitment, in marriage. True love is self-sacrifice. It takes heroes, not hotties.

God wants you to be intimately connected with others. He loves you. He accepts you no matter what mistakes you've made. And he

True love isn't just a feeling, because feelings come and go.

wants you to experience that same love and acceptance in your relationships with other people.

You're created to connect.

What would it be like to be the first and only person on earth?

> You live in an incredible garden, and you're fascinated by the place. You spend all your hours exploring because everything is new to you. Your life is full, and you're happy. Every evening you and the Creator take a walk together. You talk easily, personally.
>
> One day you peek into a pool of water and see your own reflection. You know you don't look like the animals. You wonder, Will I have a mate like the animals do? Will I have young too?
>
> So you ask the Creator about it, and the Creator says, "It is not good for man to be alone."

Okay, wait a minute, you're saying. *If God is perfect and all-knowing, why didn't he know ahead of time that the first man, Adam, needed a companion, especially when all the animals had mates?*

Good question. I believe God did know Adam would need a companion. But I think God wanted Adam to realize the importance of relationships first. To fully understand that, Adam needed to be completely alone and independent first.

You see, God couldn't complete his work in Adam until Adam experienced life *without* human companionship. That experience itself prepared him for a new relationship.

God, more than anyone else, knows your desire to be connected to another human. The Creator knew Adam wanted a mate. So what did God do for him? While Adam was sleeping, he took a rib from Adam's side and made a woman. Just imagine what it would have been like for Adam when he woke up . . .

> Adam's eyes open, then open wide. Lying next to him is the most beautiful creature he's ever seen, even more interesting

than all the animals that surround him. Oh yeah! Her body is exquisite, and it fits perfectly next to his. This has to be the mate the Creator has designed for him!

Adam's heart beats faster as he looks at her. And when she smiles as he stares into her eyes, his heart melts.

Talk about the sex drive revving into overdrive! The perfect man and the perfect woman in the most romantic garden. There was no sin or shame. Just honesty and love.

The craving for pure passion and connection still affects you more than you might think. It's how God wired you.

True Intimacy

The word *intimacy* is thrown around constantly these days. You see it in underwear ads and hear it in hot movie scenes. But is being in bed together really *intimacy?* Sure, it means the other person sees you naked. But seeing and touching another person's body do not add up to true intimacy. Without a soul-to-soul connection, sex is only lust or physical satisfaction. God has so much more for you.

True intimacy is soul-to-soul, for life. It's a depth of love that never quits.

To have that kind of relationship with another person, you first have to know what real intimacy is. And that means getting to know God. After all, how could you get more intimate than a relationship with the One who made you? When that connection "port" inside your soul—the deepest part of you—refuses to connect with God, you start to think the physical act of sex is the same as spiritual and emotional intimacy.

> True intimacy is soul-to-soul, for life.

Does Sex = Intimacy?

Have you ever heard someone say, "We fell out of love"? Baloney. You grow love. And when you remove intimacy from a growing relationship, love becomes routine. Feelings fade first, followed by the sense of closeness you once had together.

Just listen to this high schooler's story:

Last year I went out with this guy. I thought I was sooo in love, but I held out from having sex with him until about the last two or three months we saw each other. I knew we wouldn't be together again, but I wanted him to be my first, because I loved him so much. Which was SUUUCH stupid reasoning!! He was SUCH a jerk to me, he didn't deserve what I gave him!! He took something I can't ever have back—my virginity. He obviously wasn't worth it, but I, for some reason, thought he was. Don't get me wrong— we're still cool and talk when we pass in the halls. Or when I see him at a party, we'll just say hi or something. But now I have a new boyfriend, for about four months, and he's EVERYTHING I think I really deserve. He'd do anything for me. He's as in love with me as I was with my ex. . . . But it's like something's holding me back a little (having sex with my ex). I want to let go and give him my whole heart, but there's a little piece of me that just can't do that. It's killing me! . . . I'm afraid of getting hurt again— although I know my new boyfriend would never do that to me. I feel like I'm ruining the REALLY good thing I have now, with- out meaning to. And when should I tell my new boyfriend about it? Because I know he has the right to know.

—Tina, TX

Do you catch that? Her feelings about her ex flip-flop from "I knew we wouldn't be together" to "I wanted him to be my first" to "He was such a jerk to me" to "He took something" to "We're still cool and talk."

Did Tina have real intimacy or just sex?

Tina wanted acceptance and affection. She chose sex, thinking it would bring deep satisfaction. But it didn't give her what she was look- ing for. Instead it left her confused and hurting. Her soul was connected to his. Then something ripped a hole in her core. Hers appeared to be an intimate encounter—even with a jerk she knew she'd never have a lasting relationship with. However, it wasn't based on the right stuff.

And here's Genie's story:

I dated a guy for almost seven months, and recently we broke up. He's a junior and a really awesome guy. He never forced me to do anything that I didn't want to do. While we were dating, he had been in so many tragedies (deaths in the family, a tornado hitting his house) . . . and I was there for him through all of it. I am only 14, but I really do love him. And what really hurts is that he told me we would be together forever.

I figured he wouldn't know how much I love him or feel bad for him, so why not show him? So we had sex. But we didn't just have sex, we made love. I believe there is a difference. I wanted to wait for marriage, and we were going to because he'd even asked me to marry him. And then just after we made love, he was in a car wreck. I think God did that because he was telling us something. So I prayed and told God that we will never ever do that again (until marriage) if he just let us be together. I think my boyfriend wants to be with me but doesn't know how to handle everything . . . and neither do I. I need someone to help me get through this.

Genie, only 14, found a guy who promised to marry her. Because this guy had gone through so much, Genie reached out to him in compassion. He responded, and their relationship became sexual. Now she's willing to do anything, even practice abstinence, to hang on to the relationship.

Did these two high schoolers have *intimate* encounters? Physically they were intimate. But sex didn't fill their need for love and closeness. When sex enters the picture before marriage, the relationship goes downhill fast because there's no long-term commitment in place. Think about your friends, about their hit-its and quit-its. You know it's true. But this is also true: They (and you) don't have to make that choice in order to love somebody or to be loved.

> When sex enters the picture before marriage, the relationship goes downhill fast.

So if sex doesn't equal love, why is it so easy to fall into that trap?

It all began with a very sneaky creature I call *Twisted*. And he's still hard at work, trying to ruin *your* life.

3

twisted thinking
How It Got Messed Up

So what went wrong?

Eden was all about innocence and purity. No shame or guilt. No fake caring or lust. No evil.

That was your origin. Your birthplace. A place where identity was never based on how Eve looked or who Adam hung out with.

Instead, these two knew who they were because they knew God, who made them. And they knew he loved them completely. Adam and Eve could see God's fingerprints on themselves. They realized that all creation existed because of God, and they felt connected to him.

However, Adam and Eve weren't the only creatures in the Garden. Twisted was there too. Also known as Satan, he hates God and vowed to destroy the purity God had made. He's been at it for thousands of years, and now *you* are his target.

Imagine knowing someone so well that you
have nothing to hide—even if you're naked.

That was what life was like for Adam and Eve in the Garden of Eden. They were completely innocent and without sin. And they knew each other *very* well.

But something happened when they chose to sin and disobey God. If the first sin was only about eating fruit, they would have wound up with a bad case of food poisoning. Instead they realized they were naked, and shame kicked in. So they rushed to cover themselves. But they were covering more than their skin. They were trying to cover up their spiritual shame, which they became aware of only after their sin put a wall between them and God.

Do you remember as a little kid knowing you'd done something wrong and trying to hide from your parents? Somehow you thought hiding would make the shame go away. All of us have felt shame. And all of us have wanted to cover it up, to get rid of it.

Adam and Eve did the same thing. Check out 1 Corinthians 6:18 in the Bible:

> Run away from sexual sin! No other sin so clearly affects the
> body as this one does. For sexual immorality is a sin against
> your own body.

Our natural instinct when we mess up is to hide, but our attempts to hide from God keep us from having our soul's spiritual needs met.

Is it possible that there's a connection between our sexuality and our spirituality?

Is it possible that sexual sins are more powerful and more damaging than we've been told?

Is it possible that Twisted launches his best attacks at our sexual identity in order to weaken the strength of our spirit?

It's not only possible. It's fact.

Twisted was clever. Too clever for his own good, and definitely too clever for our good. Just listen to the way he weaseled Adam and Eve into going against God's orders:

> "Really?" he asked the woman. "Did God really say you must not eat any of the fruit in the garden?"
>
> "Of course we may eat it," the woman told him. "It's only the fruit from the tree at the center of the garden that we are not allowed to eat. God says we must not eat it or even touch it, or we will die."
>
> "You won't die!" the serpent hissed. "God knows that your eyes will be opened when you eat it. You will become just like God, knowing everything, both good and evil."
>
> The woman was convinced. The fruit looked so fresh and delicious, and it would make her so wise! So she ate some of the fruit. She also gave some to her husband, who was with her. Then he ate it too. At that moment, their eyes were opened, and they suddenly felt shame at their nakedness. So they strung fig leaves together around their hips to cover themselves.

When Adam and Eve chose to fall for Twisted's lies rather than to obey God, they created a ripple effect that impacts your life today. Whether you live in a broken home, suffer from an STD, are pregnant, have had an abortion, or have experienced physical or sexual abuse—or know someone who has—all of us are aware that our world is far from perfect. It all began with one bad choice. And we're responsible for whether we make similar choices in our own life.

Why did God care what Adam and Eve ate anyway?

To see how sneaky Twisted really is, try this: Simply exchange *fruit* in the story with *sex*.

> "Did God say you must not have sex at all?" the serpent asks.
>
> "Of course we can have sex," Eve replies.
> "Just not with anyone but our mate, or we will die."

"Did God say you must not have sex at all?" the serpent asks.

Hissing loudly, the serpent then screams, "You will not die! God knows that your eyes will be opened to the wonderful pleasures of sex, and the joys of your body would be yours to freely offer to others. You will know others intimately, as God does."

So Eve makes her move. A strange, new, and dark eroticism moves deep inside her as she partakes of this "fruit." Her husband beside her does the same.

Okay, so I *might* be stretching the story a bit. But I'm trying to make a point. After eating the fruit, Adam and Eve didn't just get stomachaches. The original temptation wasn't really about food. It's always been about life or death. Simply said, anything outside of God's plan brings death. The aftershocks of what seemed like such a simple act brought lifelong pain.

Twisted began his work in that garden, and you can track his evil plan all the way into your own life.

The Foundation

Okay, Doug, you're really stretching here, you may be thinking. *Sex is connected with my spiritual life?*

Absolutely. Genesis 2:18-25 says that God gave Eve to Adam. Not as an object, but as a personal and highly treasured part of Adam himself. "'At last!' Adam exclaimed. 'She is part of my own flesh and bone!'" Eve was a complete person, a separate and whole individual. When Adam accepted Eve from God, he fully validated her identity, and they were bonded for life.

God shaped Eve so she and Adam could complement each other perfectly. Then God offered her as a divine gift to Adam.

When Adam accepted Eve, he accepted her fully for who she was *physically* (their bodies uniquely connected), *spiritually* (they became one through God's actions), *emotionally* (she was exciting and balanced him), and *mentally* (he recognized her as a partner).

God created them so that when they gave themselves to each other sexually, this mutual act was a unique gift.

Accepting this gift validated and brought dignity to their masculinity and femininity. In sex, they bonded to each other in every way, not just physically.

This is the spiritual and physical foundation of our sexuality. This is what a real soul-to-soul connection looks like. This is intimacy. It's about so much more than sex.

◎

Fast-forward to today. To a world where your identity is based on what you do, where you live, what you own, and who you hang with. It's based on how sexy you are, how popular you are, how much money you have, and whether or not you've got game. Society has cheapened sex into a marketing tool.

How does Twisted attack the core foundation? He does it by making our sexuality seem only physical. He gets us to believe we are objects, that sex is only a pastime to be shared with anyone. He also convinces us that we're broken into components (physical, spiritual, and emotional) so we don't see ourselves as a whole person.

God is serious about sexual purity because sexual immorality (any sexual activity outside of marriage) betrays and destroys his design of giving and receiving for the purpose of life.

Jesus himself said, "I am the way, the truth, and the life." He also said, "I am the resurrection and the life." God is about life—exciting, satisfying, fulfilling life!

Jesus has already paid the price for anything you've done wrong. All you have to do is choose to receive this gift from him.

> How much are you worth to God? Every drop of his Son's blood.

How much are you worth to God? Every drop of his Son's blood.

A Sexy God?

I'm asking you to rethink what sex means. In a nutshell, it means *life*.

What's so bad about sex any way you get it—especially if both partners want it? Is God just trying to control the fun factor?

Far from it. God wants you to have a blast. He wants you to have the best sex possible, the way he designed it: for a lifelong marriage where both partners feel safe and loved. Anything else opens the door for messed-up families, emotional scars, and diseases (we'll talk more about STDs later). God's guidelines are for freedom. They're not there to squash the fun out of sex, but to help us see that sex—when kept in the right boundaries—is captivating and enhances a marriage relationship.

_____

God wants you to have the best sex possible.

_____

Twisted keeps busy. He constantly seduces people away from true life. He twists God-given blessings like the sex drive to fool humans into actions that cause pain and death. He's working overtime to make you miserable.

Get What You Deserve

It's about time you get what you deserve. And you deserve a pure mind, without the memories of failures and haunting sexual addictions. You deserve a pure family too, without the torn souls from divorce or the shouting matches echoing off family-room walls. He wants death.

Jesus offers the best gift to you. He died so you could have life forever with him. And he wants to make your life on earth more than you ever dreamed it could be. You deserve life.

His death on the cross and his resurrection paid the price for your failures. If you accept Jesus' payment for your sins, all your mistakes are wiped away. *All* of them. You'll be considered clean and pure again, no more guilt. And your heart will be reconnected to God's heart just as Adam's was in the Garden. Sin won't stand between you and God anymore, and your heart and mind are free to love God. And as you get to know him better and obey him, you'll want to know and love him more, just as he already knows and loves you.

Twisted's work is destructive. But a fresh start is yours for the taking.

deal with your stuff
Your Family and You

Twisted has made his mark on history. But did you know he's after you and your family too?

In a book about relationships, we've got to talk about your family members. After all, most likely they're the ones who've known you the longest. Some of you have it pretty good, all things considered. Others of you might be wondering why on earth God placed you in the family he did.

Or maybe you don't really have a family. You could be in foster care with a family you don't know well yet, one you can't quite call your own. Or maybe you feel fear, anger, and bitterness because someone in your family is verbally or physically abusive. *(If you've been abused, there's a chapter coming up just for you.)*

Why should you care?

Those of you who don't get involved in drugs, alcohol, sexual activity, and violence give *parent connectedness* as your number one reason. A study of 90,000 teens and 20,000 adults proved it.

Here's how those teens defined "parent connectedness":

- It isn't that your parents are "always there, available, sitting at home." It's that they are "available when I need them."
- It's that your mother "remembers that I had a test last Thursday and asks, 'How did it go?'"
- "It's that my father remembers that I had a date, not only that I had a date, but that it was with John and not Chris or Josh or Brandon, and asks how my date with John was."

When I ask teens why they won't have sex while they're single, many answer, "I don't want to hurt my dad." Others say, "My mom means the world to me! It would kill her."

I've written a book for your parents and other adults called *Time for a Pure Revolution*, telling them how much their attention means to you. If you want to know what I said, check out chapter 5 in that book ("What Teens Wish Parents Knew about Sex and Love").

Sure, sometimes your family will drive you crazy. But it's important to do all you can to stay connected to them. Believe it or not, those first relationships affect all the others, including your relationships with members of the opposite sex.

Melissa's Story

Melissa, a sophomore from Kansas, is one of three children. She's the "good girl" in the family who missed out on her parents' attention because they focused their time and energy on the two kids who got into trouble.

> *It seemed like I wasn't part of the family anymore. I basically had to raise myself. My parents probably figured I was smart enough to get by. But there was no more love for me in that house. It made me feel unworthy of love.*

come clean doug herman

She describes next how she went to a party and ended up having sex with a guy she'd met that night. Although she hadn't really wanted to, she slept with him. Later she told a friend how awful she felt about having sex, and the "friend" told everyone at school. The school counselor heard about it and reported it to Melissa's parents.

My mom treated me like the dirt I thought I was. It was a nightmare, and I came very close to taking my own life.

Then Melissa met another guy, and because she was so lonely, that relationship became sexual too.

I thought no one cared, I was worth nothing. At least this new guy acted like he cared. By now my parents and I were barely speaking. I had built a thick wall around myself because I was afraid if they got to know me too well they could hurt me terribly. Even more than they already had.

Melissa wanted someone to love her and pay attention to her. Her family had blown it when she opened up her heart before. Who could blame her for being afraid to risk again? Home is the most important place for receiving acceptance and love, but unfortunately it wasn't there for her.

> "My mom treated me like the dirt I thought I was."
> —Melissa

The same thing can happen when there's a death or divorce in the family. Sometimes parents aren't exactly sure how to cope either. It's easy for relationships to drift apart because being together reminds you that it isn't the same. But don't wait for your parents to come to you. Do all you can on your end to start rebuilding the bridge between you.

David's Story

David's mom died when he was six years old. He clung to his dad as they went through the funeral and the lonely months that followed.

Soon his father got busy with work, hiding his grief in his busyness. Later David's dad remarried and had two more children with his new wife. That was okay with David. In fact, he got along great with his stepmom, and having two siblings was pretty cool.

But even though they loved each other, David and his dad slowly grew apart. It wasn't until David's senior year that he and his father finally talked things through. It was a tough conversation, but they both made a commitment to work on their relationship again.

> Your relationships at home impact every relationship you'll have in the future.

"We are rebuilding the bridge to each other, beginning on our own sides," his father explained. "It's great to reconnect again and be the father my son has always wanted."

Before the Bedroom Comes the Family Room

Your relationship with your parents has a huge impact on every other relationship you will have in the future, starting with your relationships with your sisters and brothers.

The way you treat your siblings can set a pattern for how you relate to the opposite sex at school and on dates. Relationships with your brothers or sisters show you your true self, if you're willing to make the effort to notice.

Read this letter given to me by a girl named Brianna at a youth conference in Washington, D.C.

> *I have a sister who is 15. When she was a baby, she was diagnosed with Niemann-Pick disease, a rare neurological degenerative disease that affects only 500 people worldwide. I don't think I've ever really accepted the fact that one day she may be gone. I've always prayed for a miracle. But so far there's no cure. She's losing her memory, bit by bit. She trips a lot when she walks and has bad hand-eye coordination, so she can no longer take gym.*
>
> *Now that she's getting worse, I find myself at a loss. Recently, I've begun pulling away from her more and more. I'm not sure why I am pulling away from her, but I think it's 'cause I'm scared. I'm so scared she's going to die and leave me alone. I don't want to be too close to her . . . because I don't want to be*

hurt. I know that is so selfish of me! However, I know that she's my
SISTER! And she needs me and, in truth, I need her.
    Is it normal to not want to get close for fear of pain?

It's interesting how the people you love the most can also scare you the most. A part of Brianna wants to pull away from her sister now to prevent pain later. But pulling away is pain in itself.

Getting close to anyone can hurt at times, especially if that person is taken away or chooses to go away. But the rewards outweigh the risks.

To understand why family is important, just ask someone who doesn't have one. After a school assembly in New York, several students who had been adopted came up to introduce themselves to me. I asked a sophomore guy my standard question, "How young were you when you were adopted?"

> All of us want to be part of a whole.

He beamed. "Probably sixteen!"

When I raised my eyebrows in surprise, he explained, "I'm only fifteen now, but it looks like I'll get a family in a few months."

He knew the importance of family because he'd experienced life without one. It's a natural human desire to be part of a whole.

What if my parents are blowing it?

It's still *your* life we're talking about. If you see a parent making bad choices—to have an affair, to walk out on a marriage, to sleep around—it doesn't mean you have to make the same choice now or later on.

All of us will answer to God someday for the choices we make. You may not be able to change others, but you can change your own actions and thinking. You can't change your history or your parents' history, but you can change what you do from now on.

Why Try?

> You may not be able to change others, but you can change you.

Because the truth is, if you don't work on your relationships at home chances are good that unfinished business will mess up your future relationships. You have to deal with your "stuff" at home. Here are four reasons why:

#1: It's your life.

Your relationship with your family will affect every part of your life—now and in the future. After all, these people are your family, whether you love 'em or hate 'em. So pay attention to your parents; do more than just put up with your brother or sister. Get to know them.

#2: It prepares you for future relationships.

What you learn from your family will help you be more mature, interesting, and prepared for a dating relationship. When you treat your family well and keep your commitments to them, your relationships beyond the family room will be improved.

#3: You can't get rid of them.

Your parents aren't going away. Outside of a tragic accident, you'll see them every holiday for the next 30 to 40 years. They'll spoil your children as only grandparents can do, and they'll give your future spouse advice that you'll have to justify and explain later. Your parents have a huge impact on your life, the life of your future spouse, and the lives of your future children and grandchildren.

So before you ever get too serious with someone, be sure you're connecting with your family first.

They're the relationships you need before the relationship you want.

#4: Your family background affects your identity and self-esteem.

The messages you've picked up from your parents and siblings over the years affect your opinion of yourself. We all have a natural tendency to search for relationships that fill emotional needs that weren't met as children. If your father was cold and unaffectionate, you may feel a strong pull to date an affectionate person. But if you mistake physical affection for love, you could be fooled into one of Twisted's traps and try to fill that need with sex.

> Family: They're the relationships you need before the relationship you want.

The more whole and healthy you are emotionally *before* dating, the more you'll stick to high standards for yourself. When a person feels good about herself, she's less likely to settle for shabby treatment from others.

Reconnect... with You

Sometimes you don't know yourself as well as you think you do.

Surprised?

It's important to reconnect with your family members. But what about yourself? Do *you* really know yourself? What does figuring that out have to do with relationships?

Unless you know who you are, you can never be ready for a satisfying relationship with someone else. A "half" person does not bring enough to make a whole relationship.

And the truth is, the only way to really understand and accept yourself is to get to know the One who made you. So let's get down to it . . .

What's your purpose?

Ask yourself this question: "Why am I breathing?" You see, God created you for a reason. There are things set in advance for you to accomplish in life. Do you know why you exist? why you breathe? Your answer is your purpose in life.

Several teens at a youth retreat were asked what their purpose was. These were some of their initial answers: to be popular, to drive a car, to get married. But they soon realized that they needed a larger vision for their lives than that. Their focus was too narrow. The experience of rethinking their purpose caused them to find something "bigger" to live for.

Take a moment to think about your purpose and jot down a list of what comes to mind.

Then ask yourself, *Does what I'm doing now match up with the life goals I just wrote down?*

Don't Settle

If you're looking for a great relationship but you offer sex to your dates, it's not likely you're going to find that guy or girl who loves you for who you are. Your current lifestyle is not leading you toward your life goals. You do get what you put in. Hold on to your life goals, and remember that self-respect raises the standards you live by. God wants a clean life for you. Don't settle for anything less.

Staying Clean

Do you know your greater purpose in life?

If you have decided to hang on to sexual purity but you haven't nailed down your reasons yet, look at your life goals. In order to have a life free of the emotional and physical pain that sex outside of marriage brings, stick to your goals. Refuse to compromise those goals for a date. You don't need to do that to be loved. Be selfish with yourself. You deserve the relationship that God has planned for you.

The Creator of the world and our body has called us to this battle for clean lives.

> God wants you to be holy, so you should keep clear of all sexual sin. Then each of you will control your body and live in holiness and honor—not in lustful passion as the pagans do, in their ignorance of God and his ways. . . . God has called us to be holy, not to live impure lives.

The road will not be easy. At some point you'll probably face huge sexual temptations. You'll want to please the guy or girl you're with. You'll wonder if you're just being a prude. But God has made his position clear, and he wants you to be bold about your stand: "For God has not given us a spirit of fear and timidity, but of power, love, and self-discipline."

Does pure equal perfect?

If you choose to be pure, does that mean you'll be perfect? that you'll never think about sex? Nope. Saying no will be difficult, especially if you've had sex before. But it's not impossible. Remember, Twisted is working against you, and he's dying to see you fall on your face.

So when you struggle, turn to God first. Ask him to keep your mind and your heart clean. Tell Jesus that you want him to remove anything that's impure from you. Ask him to help you relate to people in ways that are pleasing to him. Then you won't be sorry down the road.

Being pure is a struggle for most people, especially when we're surrounded by a society that's selling sex. Here are five steps to help you stay clean.

Step #1: Ask for forgiveness.
Ask God to forgive you for your failures. He can, and he wants to. Accepting his forgiveness won't mean your struggles will magically go away. But God will cleanse you and help you grow stronger if you ask him to.

Step #2: Be real with yourself and others.
Look into those dark, hidden corners of your heart—the places you don't want to venture into because you're afraid of who or what you might find there. Be completely honest with God and yourself. And be honest with someone you trust to challenge you to grow. Ask God to show you the real you. God knows you inside out anyway, and he's waiting to step into your zone. You don't have to clean yourself up before you talk with him, because it's impossible to do that by yourself. He'll work in you if you let him.

God is waiting to step into your zone.

Step #3: Change your lifestyle.
I hate diets. You know why? They're temporary. The pounds eventually come back. That is, unless you *change your lifestyle.*

The same applies for living a clean life. Instead of drifting in and out of the pure life, change your lifestyle. If you find yourself looking at porn magazines or Web sites, lock yourself out of those sites. Make sure you're only on the computer when your mom or dad is home. Try going on group dates in busy places instead of quiet, romantic locations. Or say no to the whole dating scene for a while until you can gain some backbone.

You can change your lifestyle if you're committed to.

Step #4: Guard yourself.

If you were Twisted, how would you attack yourself to try to destroy you?

This is a question I've asked many teens. You're smart—you know your own weaknesses. No one really *falls* into sin; we step into it. Since you know your weaknesses, you know how the enemy will probably attack you.

So why not prepare for it in advance? If you can't say no to alcohol, take a friend who doesn't drink to a party with you. If your mind

---
No one falls into sin; we step into it.

---

spins with thoughts about sex, change the channel in your brain. Ask a trustworthy friend or adult to ask you the tough questions to help you stay on track.

Step #5: Reconnect with those who care.

On your road to coming clean, you'll need people to encourage you. We already talked about your parents and siblings. Here are a couple of other good places to look to for support.

School. Studies show that students do better in school if they feel valued there. They also get involved in fewer risky activities. Flex your muscles. Get involved with school activities or student government and be a part of positive changes.

Church or youth group. If you're already connected to a local church or youth group, great! Why not go beyond the youth ministry and volunteer to work with children, do drama, or help with the elderly? God created you with unique gifts and passions, and you can make a big difference. You'll also learn more about God during the time you spend at church activities. If you aren't part of a church, why not get involved in one or find a mentor?

God is absolutely crazy about you. His love for you is so intense that he's gone to the greatest lengths possible to offer you a personal relationship with himself. And his plan for your life is a perfect fit for you. Get to know him. The more you know him, the more clearly you'll understand his plan.

When you reconnect with yourself, your parents, your school, your church, and with God, you can't help but become stronger and more joyful.

> God is absolutely crazy about you.

Stand strong. The battle is not over. Accept God's forgiveness. Be honest with yourself. Realize your weaknesses, and guard yourself from attack in those areas by changing your lifestyle.

Dig deep inside. You *can* come clean and stay that way.

5

know the no
You Are Worth Waiting For

Let's be honest: No one likes to wait!

So you get this book, or a speaker comes to your school or youth group and simply says, "Don't have sex!" What happens next?

A roar of laughter!

Then the speaker says, "Don't have sex . . . yet. You can have tons of sex . . . but not until you're married." What happens next?

Snickers . . . but some listen and agree.

Wherever I go, I expect mixed responses—especially since I'm saying not only no sex, but also no genital contact of any kind. And all this in a world where sex is cheap and easy, and we're surrounded by images of sexiness on all sides.

Most teens have strong sexual drives raging within them.

And that's natural. God created us with those drives. Having them isn't wrong; it's what we do with them that can be right or wrong.

Battles of the Sexes and the Exes

Whether it's the battle of the sexes or the battle of the exes, we love to love, and love to hate those we used to love.

God created us with those sexual drives. Having them isn't wrong; it's what we do with them that can be right or wrong.

Many of you are involved in relationships right now. The emotions can be quite powerful. "If I don't have sex with him, I might lose him. And he's a great guy!" I sense what you're feeling in that statement. But instead of listening to what I might say, listen to some of your peers who've been there:

> *Two years ago my boyfriend at the time made me have intercourse with him. (It wasn't really rape, because we had been talking about it for some time then.) But he made me think it was right for me to do it, because it would make him happy. It took me nine months to get out of that relationship, and I finally realize that even though he said he loved me, it wasn't for who I was.*
>
> *I now have a boyfriend who I know loves me for WHO I am, not my appearance, because he doesn't care about the sexual stuff with me. He knows everything that has happened to me in my past, and he doesn't hold it against me. He's my best friend, and he is always there for me. We've been together for a year, and this is the happiest I have ever been. I know I love this guy. It may not be the type of marriage love, but I love him for who he is.*
>
> —Savannah, OH

Savannah found out what is most important. If only she could have seen into the future, or at least down the road a bit. I hope that if they are to be together, they make sure they both understand the consequences of past actions. Is it possible the one *you* are now dating may not be the one you spend your life with?

Yeah, having sex is a very powerful experience. Not only is it a way to show how much you love each other, but it bonds you intensely. That's why breakups after being sexually involved hurt so much . . . and why some people get insanely jealous as well. Did you know that the average high school relationship lasts only three weeks after the first sexual experience?

The average high school relationship lasts only three weeks after the first sexual experience.

The sex drive is a gift from God. But to give in to that drive before commitment places your couple status on thinner ice. And until the marriage license is signed, sealed, and delivered so to speak, don't do it.

There's a very simple test that shows if your relationship is based on sex or not. Here it is: *stop the sex*. If the relationship falls apart, it was based on the physical. If it gets better, why ruin it and add sex again? Let it get better. Perhaps it will grow to become permanent with the right person.

To test your relationship's depth, stop the sex.

Even in the movie *How to Lose a Guy in 10 Days*, the guy realizes that in order to get a relationship to last, he'd have to hold off on sex. And that was a guy who wasn't concerned about God's views on the subject. So if the average male "player" knows that early sex means an early end to a relationship, then why do it? It's better to wait—to not have sex or to stop having sex—and let the relationship grow from there.

How about . . . NO?

No one can make you do something stupid. You have to jump into "stupid" yourself. To know better and to jump into a risky activity is . . . well, stupid. When you have the ability to choose, not making a choice is still a choice. In other words, "letting it happen" in the backseat if you're able to prevent it is also your choice. And every choice has a consequence.

No one can make you do something stupid. You have to jump into "stupid" yourself.

How do I say no?
Simple. Don't get to the point when that decision has to be made at the last minute. It's better to have that discussion before you even hold hands! Set your limits and stick to them. Even when your heart is pounding and your mind is swimming with intoxicating ideas and images, *stop*.

But I'll be even more real. If you do decide to kiss, keep it under five minutes. Otherwise it only sets you up for more arousal and a tougher situation that requires hitting the brakes.

More real than that? Okay. If you do find yourself in a hot 'n' heavy situation, you may hear that little voice of conscience in your head. You need to stop, but how? CHANGE something! Change the music, change your location (like get out of the car), or even change the images racing through your head.

Tell the other person you care about them and yourself and want to stop. Of course, they may not agree. Some have every argument perfected:

- It's because we love each other that we feel this way. Why stop our love?
- If you really cared about me, you'd prove it to me.
- I've thought for years about who would be my first. No one in my life will get this gift but you. Why won't you accept this gift from me?
- I thought we were a mature couple. What's the problem?
- It's not like you're a virgin (if you've been sexually active before). So why are you taking this out on me?
- We've talked about this before. We have a connection; it's special. Since our hearts are connected, what's wrong with hooking up?

And my "favorite":

- God created sex. He gave you and me the feelings we both feel for each other right now. This is a good thing, not something bad, so let's enjoy it. I know we talked about marriage . . . and I do want to marry you. But what is a piece of paper compared to what we feel now?

What do you do when someone gives you these lines as a reason to have sex? Think of it this way: Your date isn't really listening to what you said. You said you wanted to stop. Instead of honoring that wish and showing self-control by putting *you* first, your date is trying to change your mind. Since he or she refuses to honor your wishes and standards, waste no more time. Leave! Just get up and walk away. No big explosion or fanfare, just remove yourself. You can talk about it later when the emotions aren't so intense.

True Love, True Men

Guys, let's be men. It's not the girl's job to be the emergency brake in a relationship. It's not her responsibility to tell you how far is too far. If you're a true man of strength and honor, you won't lead a girl into a situation where she'd have to say no to you.

The firefighters of New York City understood self-sacrifice during the 9/11 tragedy. Many of them died trying to save complete strangers. Jesus was about self-sacrifice too. He was innocent, yet he hung on a cross and endured a brutal death for you. He's the ultimate hero.

Your commitment to control and master your very powerful sexual urges shows the strength of your manhood.

If someone isn't willing to sacrifice their desires for your wishes, they don't truly love you. And they don't deserve you. So leave. Change. Move. Speak. Kick, maybe. But don't just stay there and "let it happen."

A Word to Your Lover

If you had to write something today to your future spouse, what would you write? Would you share your dreams? thoughts of your future careers, your house, pets, vacations, names of your future children? What would you say, really?

Go ahead and write that person a short letter to share whatever's on your heart.

Someday you'll be with someone who loves you so much that they'll give their very life for you and devote themselves to you alone. How exciting! Why not start a continuing letter or journal to your future spouse now, *before you even meet him or her*? When the time is right, you may want to give those letters or journals as a gift, letting this person know how you've been devoted to him or her even before you met.

Now, if you knew you were going to write your future spouse a letter the *same weekend* you were going to prom, would it affect your actions during the night of prom? It did for Yolanda.

You spoke to our school the week of prom. Thank you so much for your message. Your talk is the number one reason I am still a virgin today. I don't know how to thank you enough.

—*Yolanda, MI*

Your letter might say, *"I'm going out tonight . . . and I hope it's you I'm going out with . . . but whether it is or not, I want you to know I'll be faithful to you."*

Impressive.

A Case for Character

Since you're thinking about what your future spouse will be like, let's talk about this person's heart and soul. What kind of guy or girl are you waiting for? What will others think of him or her?

Great character—what someone is like on the inside—is a non-negotiable in relationships that last.

Character means not changing yourself for somebody else, or at least that is what good character is. People who change themselves for others are usually not honest with themselves. I choose my friends by how I hope they choose their friends: for the people they are and not for who they are with. I think if we choose friends with a solid foundation and strong character, we will surround ourselves with good influences and become better people as we spend time together.

—*Lance, FL*

Don't you wish people could love and respect you for *who you are,* not for your actions, your body rating, or your grades? If you value someone only for what you can see, you've missed it. Too many times

come clean doug herman

quality people are overlooked or belittled because of how others judge them based on their physical appearance.

Every time I deal with this issue of inner beauty in public schools, I see the smiles and grins coming from students with great insides. Many are completely healthy. But nothing energizes me more than sharing this message when there are students in wheelchairs on the sides of the gym or the auditorium. They too want to be loved for who they are, not for what they can or can't do physically. It's about the soul!

Thank you, thank you for speaking! Some people see my girlfriend and ask her why I like her since she's "not pretty." But I tell her, "You are gorgeous." People don't understand that I love her for who she is and not what she looks like.

—Xavier, AZ

Real love is never based on sex, feelings, or the bedroom. Real love is grown and developed between two people over time. It takes time to get to know someone. You cannot get to know someone through a one-night stand, under an alcohol-induced buzz, or from only a few months of dating.

It's really hard to find a guy who will respect me for me, not just because of how I look. I haven't had a relationship in a couple of years. Kinda gets lonely . . . but I know he's out there somewhere!

—Lorena, TX

This Texan girl reminds me of another teen from my youth group several years ago. She was beautiful to the point that she often scared guys off. But she was very picky about who she dated. She was very careful to date only those who took the time to get to know the real her first. With such a high standard, she often wasn't dating anybody. But she wasn't lonely. Those times taught her to be content with herself without needing a guy.

I lost my father to AIDS when I was seven and can't talk about it very well. I am in a serious long-term relationship now with someone I am very much in love with. I know it's odd to find your soul mate when you are only 15, but I have—and I could never be happier. I'm not going to go into detail on how far she and I have gone, but after what you said about real love, it really made me think. I have totally reshaped the time I spend with her (every Sunday) and my love for her.

—John, NY

I want to wait and save my love for my husband and not just some guy. I'm not saying my current boyfriend is just some guy, but I don't really know what the future has in store for me. I'm just trying to take it one day at a time.

—Cindy, WA

Love is an expression of your whole being. Saving yourself doesn't mean only your virginity. It involves your heart and mind and your spirit and soul. Saving this love for your future spouse shows big-time maturity.

Love Me for ME!

Sharon, a young girl from Tulsa, wrote this poem following my presentation at her school. I wanted to share it with you since it captures so well what I'm trying to say.

Deeper Than Skin
Beauty is the strangest thing
In this world that we live in.
You can have the world on a string
If the beauty is as deep as skin.

But older, older we must grow
And certainly in time,

Our true heart begins to show
And our beauty begins to shine.

Not many people understand
Until they stop and think
They look only at the shell of man
And their spirits start to sink.

They realize that they've been wrong
Until this final day.
Each person sings their lovely song
In their own special way.

But you have known this all along
You help us all to see.
You teach us all and make us strong
You're as beautiful as can be!

You're wonderful and special—thanks for teaching us that we are too!

My youngest children have several great sitters. One of those girls was discussing this idea of loving and being loved for who you are, not what you look like or what you can do sexually. She writes:

When I look for someone to be in a relationship with, the two most important things to find are someone who likes me for me and someone who won't force me to go further sexually than I want to. I want to find someone who will look past my physical appearance and actually see what's on the inside. Someone who will like me for my inner beauty instead of the outer. Someone who will love me when I get older, even if I become the ugliest person in the world. Finding someone who will respect me for what I want to do and what I don't want to do in a relationship means a lot to me. I think that respecting yourself and what you want in a relationship is the most important thing.

—Melissa, CO

But sometimes, when we look in the mirror, we question even *our own* value. Maybe we don't see much of anything we're proud of. Or if we've made bad decisions or had negative experiences in the past—we feel secondhand and of less worth . . . or completely worthless. What do we do then?

A Fight to Remain Clean

If you look at yourself and say, "But, Doug! I'm not clean!" I say welcome to humanity! Name one person without a past.

Romans 3:23 says, "All have sinned; all fall short of God's glorious standard." *No one* is worthy of God's love and purity. Now, that would be depressing—except for the truth that follows. Romans 5:8 says that even *while we were sinners,* "God showed his great love for us by sending Christ to die for us." Through his death and resurrection, we are offered eternal life. He paid the price of death for every failure you ever committed or will commit in the future.

How do you cash in on that payment for your sins? Simply let Jesus become your God. Realize you can never be perfect and clean inside on your own. Ask Jesus to remove the stains of your past, and decide to follow his direction from now on.

That is the only way to come clean with God. We can never be good enough, nice enough, or pure enough by our own efforts. We are sinners. But through the grace of God, every failure—and those sins committed against you—can be washed away. It doesn't matter how much you say you've messed up. God still chooses to love you and forgive you. The only question is, *Will you let him?*

If your answer is yes, then spend a moment and speak to him as you would to your friend. Try a simple prayer like this:

> *Dear God,*
>
> *This feels sort of strange, but I know you are real. I can sense you. And I feel so inadequate. Please forgive me for my failures. I want to start over today. From this day on, I want you to be in charge of my life. I choose you as my God right now. I'll do what you want. Thanks for having your Son, Jesus, pay the price for my sins. Now*

help me to do something with my life to help others as well. Guide me there. Amen.

Words don't cleanse you, but true confession from the heart does. God purifies your heart from sin and gives you a new chance. Your goal is to discipline your life toward perfection and trust God to help you. It's a tough challenge but a worthy one, and one you have the ability to meet.

What happens if you mess up? Well, God knew before he saved you that you would. But he saved you anyway. You don't have to perform to be loved by your Creator. You just have to be yourself and be honest. If you mess up, don't quit. Simply ask God to forgive you and cleanse you. Connect with friends, family, a youth group leader, or a minister to help you change your lifestyle. Then get right back up and keep trying. You deserve this clean start for your future.

what's it gonna cost me?

The Price of High-risk Sex

The Consequences

Let's recap. So far we've established that (1) sex is everywhere, (2) God had an original plan for sex, (3) the original plan got messed up, and (4) your family plays an important role in identity and purity issues.

This chapter takes a more in-depth look at three of the four consequences of high-risk sexual activity: pregnancy, relational and emotional pain, and the impact on your character and future. We'll talk about the fourth and deadliest consequence in the next chapter.

Consequence #1: Pregnancy

A few weeks ago my boyfriend and I had unprotected sex numerous times. One day I got out of the shower and felt really dizzy and sick to my stomach. He came and sat down by me and asked what was wrong, I told him that I was feeling really sick, like throwing-up sick. He got real quiet and said, "I hope I didn't get you pregnant!" I got really scared. So did he.

—Anne, CO

The first and obvious consequence is pregnancy. Every year nearly 900,000 girls under 20 get pregnant in the United States.

In our nation, if a girl is pregnant, she has three legal options: She can parent the baby, abort the child, or place that child for adoption.

A pregnant teen has three options.

Yes, she and her boyfriend had a choice before: "Should I have sex or not?" Now though, after the fact, her choices are much different. And the choice she makes will affect her not only physically and relationally, but also emotionally, for the rest of her life.

Option #1: Parent the baby.

This *can* be a good choice, but it's definitely not an easy one. A support network made up of family, church, youth group, school, and friends is hugely important. But that's usually not the situation.

While I was in southwest Georgia, I did 15 high school assemblies in different schools. I was amazed at how many teen moms and pregnant girls—from seventh grade to high school seniors—approached me. Each girl had a tough road ahead. "I have two kids," one senior shared. "And you're right, it *is* hard."

Teen parents face many hurdles. Only half finish high school because of the stress in their lives and the time spent taking care of a baby. As a result, nearly 80 percent of teen mothers live at or below the poverty line. That means if you were to have a baby now, chances are in a few years you'd be living on food stamps as you send your son or daughter off to kindergarten. And imagine trying to rake together savings for your child's college tuition on an income from McDonald's.

Teen mothers are also more likely to remain single for most of their children's early years. Why? Because few teen fathers stick around after hearing the words "I'm pregnant." The reality is that only 20 to 30 percent of teen fathers actually marry their baby's mother.

That means most of these girls raise their child without the help and support of a father. Most are still unmarried five years after having the baby. Instead of hanging out with friends, going to parties, and playing sports, a teen mother spends her time changing diapers, waking up for late-night feedings, and wiping drippy noses.

> Only 20 to 30 percent of teen fathers actually marry their baby's mother.

I would like to ask those guys what they believe being there for the girl really means. Yeah, it's easy to be there during the pregnancy, baby showers, the birth, and the first months. But the glory runs out when the responsibility and the inevitable exhaustion kick in. Some guys have told me they're willing to pay child support for those 18 years—that it's a responsibility they're willing to bear. But running from that mother and child to hide in a career and send an occasional check is hardly being there.

Studies show that children of teen mothers are more likely to have low math and reading scores, repeat grades, have sex before age 16, fight at school or work, and skip school.

An eighth-grade girl once told me, "I *want* to have a baby. Because I want the baby to love me." This girl was so lacking love in her life that she'd fallen for one of Twisted's lies.

Having a child is not the way to find love. Love is all about self-sacrifice, not about warm feelings. Jesus himself said, "Here is how to measure it—the greatest love is shown when people lay down their lives for their friends." In order to raise a child well, you've got to "lay down" your life. You must sacrifice your comfort, other commitments, time, and sleep for your baby. And it isn't over until that child is an adult.

Option #2: Abort the baby.
Years ago I thought that abortion was wrong except in extreme cases like incest, rape, or if the unborn baby is somehow threatening the life of the mother. You may believe that too. My opinion did a 180 when I met Pam Stenzel.

Pam's mother was only 15 when she was raped. She became pregnant, but instead of choosing abortion, she carried the baby to term and then placed the child for adoption. Pam was adopted, and she has reached thousands with her life and message.

I was spellbound as I watched this intelligent woman speak at a high school in Minnesota. Everyone held their breath as she shared her story. She bluntly told the 1,500 students, "My father is a rapist. I don't even know my nationality. Do you really think my life is worth less than yours because of how I was conceived?" She paused, and the silence in the gym was deafening. "I didn't deserve the death penalty for some crime my father committed."

So is abortion a *right* or a *choice*? Some would argue that it is your body, and therefore your right. But the Bible says that God knows us before we are conceived or formed in the womb. So our soul exists before conception, meaning there's life before birth.

Roughly 3,000 abortions occur every day in America. Imagine subtracting 3,000 people from your high school or your graduating class.

Abortion has become quite a business. It can seem like an easy Band-Aid to avoid negative reactions from family and friends or to keep from messing up college plans.

I want to be clear here. I am compassionate toward those who have had abortions—including some good friends of mine.

But I also believe in being honest. Just because someone doesn't like the consequence doesn't give that person the right to eliminate another life. Especially when God says that every life is precious and that he sees and watches over every baby in the womb: "You watched me as I was being formed in utter seclusion, as I was woven together in the dark of the womb. You saw me before I was born. Every day of my life was recorded in your book. Every moment was laid out before a single day had passed."

There is some good news for unborn babies. In the United States, abortion rates have continued to go down since 1990. That means your generation is making more informed choices than the generation before you. You have a regard for life—and that is something to celebrate.

> So is abortion a right or a choice?

Option #3: Place the baby for adoption.

I love talking with students who've been adopted. I want to meet them in person. "You are a chosen child," I tell them. "That makes you special." A ninth grader wrote me this letter after we met:

> *I've never met my real parents, but I know my mother was a teenager when she got pregnant, so that's why I was put up for adoption. But I guess I am very fortunate because I was adopted by the best set of parents I could possibly ask for. The only thing I didn't like about being adopted is that I always felt kind of singled out or different from everybody else. After you talked to us, I felt so much better about being adopted.*

—Faith, TX

Placing a baby for adoption is not an easy choice. It takes special strength, knowledge, and determination to follow through with it. A young girl has to decide to carry the baby full term, which means experiencing all the discomforts of pregnancy. She also feels every movement of the child and experiences a special bond. Then she gives birth to the child, knowing she will not be there when that baby smiles, says "Mama," or graduates from high school. Placing a baby for adoption brings with it deep and immediate loss for a young mother.

Many students have told me sadly that they were "given away" by parents or families who must not have wanted them. So I tell them Rachel's story.

She was 15 years old and seven-and-a-half-months pregnant when I met her in northwest Ohio, where she was staying in a home for pregnant teenagers. As other girls around the circle shared stories, most talked about how they planned to keep their babies. Most had found the fathers not as dependable as the girls had initially thought. When we finally came to Rachel, she placed her hand on her growing belly.

"Mr. Herman, you need to understand something," she began, tears forming in her blue eyes. "I can't raise this baby. I don't have a family that supports me. And I don't have the money. I don't even know who the father is." The tears now raced down her cheeks and her long curly hair snagged in wet lines. "You may want to raise your child," she told the other girls, "and that's cool. But I can't. I really want this baby to have a happy family and a great future. But it won't find that with me. This baby deserves better."

> **"I don't want to give this baby away—I want to give it a chance." —Rachel, pregnant at 15**

Compassion softened her eyes. "I don't want this baby to ever think I gave it away. But I want it to have a family, a future, and hope. Mr. Herman, I don't want to give this baby away—I want to give it a chance."

You were not given away . . . you were given a chance. That's a lifelong gift.

Sadly, less than one percent of pregnant teens choose adoption.

If you're pregnant and considering adoption, you should be aware of the emotions you will go through during and after the birth. Know that your heart will bond with that baby. It's important to talk through the process with your parents. Connecting with a supportive family, whether it's your own or another that supports you, can make all the difference—not only in the process of adoption itself, but also for your emotional and physical health.

Consequence #2: Relational and Emotional Pain

There's another reason not to have sex yet—a big, compelling reason.

> **"They don't make a condom big enough to cover the human heart."**

Lakita Garth, a friend of mine and a fellow speaker, has said, "They don't make a condom big enough to cover the human heart." Sadly, I've seen the truth of that played out in hundreds of thousands of teens' lives across the country.

Low Expectations?

Imagine the scene at home as I leave for a speaking engagement:

"Sweetheart, I'm leaving!" I shout to my wife, Stephanie.

Running up to me with one of the kids' half-folded shirts in hand, she offers me a kiss. "I love you, honey," she says. We hug. Although I love my work, it's always hard to leave my family.

"I need to go," I say, kissing her again.

Then I grab my bags and open the door.

Stephanie turns me to face her one last time and says, "Honey, remember, I'm your wife."

"Of course I'll remember. How can I forget?"

"I want you to be faithful to me."

Somewhat taken aback, I blink hard and say nothing for a moment. "Uh . . . of course I'll be faithful, honey."

"But just in case you aren't, take these," she says, handing me a box of condoms.

Of course that's *not* how it happens. My wife and I are committed to each other, and that commitment includes respect, honor, and self-discipline.

But that kind of scene does happen in most school health classes. By handing you condoms as you run out the door, adults are expecting you to be unfaithful to yourself and your future spouse and unable to control your sex drive. That sends the message that you don't have self-respect or strength. Don't buy it! You have as much ability to be strong and controlled as any married person—perhaps more so—and you deserve respect and trust.

The consequences of relational and emotional betrayal are immense—both now and in the future. The dating scene is so intense that many teens go through deep depression after a breakup. Statistics show high depression and suicide rates among sexually active students. Many high school relationships today have the factors of a marriage without the commitment. But without commitment and self-sacrifice—parts of true love—the relationship won't last.

> Without commitment and self-sacrifice—parts of true love—the relationship won't last.

If you have sex before you're married, you're forced to believe one of two lies to avoid getting hurt: Either you can disconnect with your emotions to keep from feeling anything, or you can view sex as nonemotional—only physical entertainment. One Web site for teens says, "*Love* can mean many different things to many different people. Sex, on the other hand, is a biological event."

In most schools you're taught that you're essentially an animal at your core, only more complex. You've probably heard of "sport sex" and "friends with benefits." It's only a physical act, right?

If that's true, how will you recognize true friendship and true love? And if you get married someday, what foundation are you building to stay faithful? When a marriage is healthy, both people benefit physically, emotionally, and spiritually. Are you training yourself for divorce?

It's not possible to separate emotion from what you do with your body. You will feel something—someday.

After a recent assembly I gave in Texas, Sally wrote me this letter:

> *I never talk to anyone about things I consider personal, and I shocked myself by telling you about [my drug use]. I really enjoyed speaking to you. That came as another surprise to me because I like how it feels not to feel. That is one of my reasons for using. It's easier to live that way, but I know (from experience) that's not really living.*

People can only take so much pain. If they can't find healing, they will find an escape. Sally began using drugs at age 12 to cover her pain from sexual experiences. Since then she's tried heroin and ecstasy; currently she's using prescription drugs including Vicodin. Sally is trying to escape her pain, and she knows it. But she's afraid to stop using drugs, because she *likes how it feels not to feel.*

But if you're in this situation, you can find help from a pastor or priest. Crisis pregnancy centers' doors ring as young women enter their offices, looking for someone to guide them through the tangled messes they're in. A doctor or therapist can also give guidance.

Consequence #3: The Impact on Your Character and Future

What are your friends like? No one enjoys spending time with a person whose first priority is herself. A good friend has character and personality—what's inside is what counts.

Think about your own character. You can never go wrong with faithfulness, self-control, and goodness—all fruits of the Spirit. Especially in today's world, where everybody seems to be out for themselves.

If you're involved in sports, you know physical training is essential to becoming a better athlete. Take weight lifting for example: You lie down on a narrow bench as a teammate places weights on the bar above you. You have to resist the pressure, and sometimes it's pretty painful. But when you succeed, you feel awesome. No pain, no gain! Training makes you *stronger*.

It's the same with sex. Anyone can have sex. Big deal. But to become strong, you've got to face the pressure. Then you have to resist that pressure. With continued success in the "wait room," you become stronger than ever.

> To become strong, you've got to face the pressure. Then you have to resist it.

If you want your future spouse to be faithful, you need to know they've exercised those muscles that say, "No. I'm not having sex until I'm married." Otherwise, how can you be sure your husband or wife won't leave you for someone else down the road? You deserve someone with strength, not weakness.

No one deserves the painful consequences you've read about in this chapter. Your future is your choice. And it begins with the choices you make today.

Every choice has a consequence.

You can step into Twisted's trap and let him damage your life. Or you can choose God's way. You can start over. No matter what your past has been, it's never too late to change your life, your attitude, and your actions for your own good.

You're a player in the game of love. It's your body. It's your soul and emotions. And it's your future at stake.

It's your choice.

7

what goes around comes around
The Real Facts about STDs

Imagine standing by your best friend's side as she is dying....
That's exactly what I had to do with my late wife, Evon, who was also my best friend. For 70 minutes I watched her struggle for air as her pulse rate went from 78 to 188 to 0. On September 9, 1991, she took her last breath.

My wife did not have a choice in contracting the STD that killed her. It came to her through a blood transfusion. Neither did my daughter Ashli. It came to her through birth. But all across this nation I've met adults and teens who are dying just like Evon and Ashli did, *by choice*. And for what? For one hour of sex on a Friday night or after prom. For sex games after school.

The fourth consequence, and the topic of this chapter, is STDs. Get ready for a reality check.

That's gonna leave a mark!

Do you remember the comedy *Tommy Boy*, starring Chris Farley? He was constantly hitting his head on something and grunting, "That's gonna leave a mark!" We laughed at the comedy because it isn't real and it doesn't give *us* a headache.

But there are actions some of us take that *will* leave a mark. A mark that can't be erased or reversed.

A woman can get pregnant only three to six days a month, depending on her cycle. But girls and guys can contract an STD *any* day of the month. Unlike pregnancy, which requires intercourse, STDs don't require intercourse or penetration. Each year over 15 million Americans, including approximately 4 million teenagers, are infected with STDs. And the number is growing. In 1996 one in four sexually active people had an STD. In 2003 one in three 25-year-olds had STDs! And two-thirds of STDs occur in people college-age or younger. That means you and your peers are definitely fair game.

Doctors believe the growing numbers are because people are having sex at a younger age, the divorce rate is higher, and people are getting married later. More sexual partners increases the risk of STDs—and many of those diseases have no noticeable symptoms.

So people who are infected continue to pass on the disease because they don't know they have it.

Teens are at high risk for acquiring STDs because they're "more likely than other age groups to have multiple sex partners, to engage in unprotected sex, and, for younger women, to choose sexual partners older than themselves," says America's Centers for Disease Control and Prevention (CDC).

> Some STDs are curable. Others are not.

So what are sexually transmitted diseases (STDs) or sexually transmitted infections (STIs), as some people are now calling them? They can be put into two general categories: *bacterial* infections and *viral* infections. One is curable; the other is not. I only have room to give you the highlights—or lowlights.

Bacterial Infections

Bacterial infections are caused by bacteria and are treatable and curable.

But treatments can't guarantee that there won't be problems later. Worse, young women are biologically more susceptible to chlamydia, gonorrhea, and HIV because of the cervix and its development. Let's start with chlamydia and gonorrhea, the two most common curable STDs among teens.

Chlamydia

Chlamydia is the most commonly reported infectious disease in the United States. The Center for Disease Control in Atlanta believes it's also one of the most dangerous STDs among women today because three-quarters of chlamydia infections in women don't show symptoms. Half of the men infected don't know they are. And so this STD spreads easily. Here's the rundown:

- If untreated, 40 percent of women with chlamydia will develop pelvic inflammatory disease (PID).
- One in five women with PID becomes infertile.
- Chlamydia also can cause prematurity, eye disease, and pneumonia in infants.
- Women infected with chlamydia are three to five times more likely to become infected with HIV, if exposed.

Gonorrhea

What about gonorrhea?

- Gonorrhea is a major cause of PID and subsequent infertility in women, as well as tubal pregnancies (when a fertilized egg implants in the fallopian tube instead of in the uterus).
- Both men and women may experience infertility plus infection in their joints, heart valves, or brain.
- Infected people also run a greater risk of HIV infection if they are exposed.
- Unborn and newborn babies may suffer blindness, meningitis (inflammation of the membranes that envelop the brain and the spinal cord), and septic arthritis (inflammation of joints caused by infection).

Viral Infections

Viral infections, caused by a virus, are very different from bacterial infections. Their *symptoms* may be treatable, but the infection can't be cured. Will there ever be a cure for viral STDs such as HIV? Recent reports of vaccination for specific strains of some viral STDs look encouraging. But still, these are not cures. While they help prevent future infections, they cannot kill a virus once it's inside your body.

Because viral infections are so serious and incurable, let's talk about the four that most commonly affect the people at your school.

Genital Herpes

Meet Shaniqua

Of the thousands of assemblies I've presented, few have impacted me like one at a high school in Texas. As the principal made his closing remarks, a freshman girl named Shaniqua came up to me and introduced herself. Then she asked, "Mr. Herman, do you think I will find someone who will love me . . . for me? Not for what I look like physically, but for who I am on the inside, as a person?"

I began to reply quickly with a yes, but she cut me off. "Even . . . even if I have to tell him that I have herpes?"

I squeezed her hand. "I believe there are men in this community—even in this school—who have enough character to love you for who you are. Even if you have to tell him you have herpes. Yes, I believe he's out there."

Her eyes began watering. "Thanks," she choked out. Then she added, "But I wish . . . I wish you'd been here . . . before."

"Me too," I whispered. My eyes burned with tears as she turned to walk down the auditorium aisle.

Shaniqua contracted genital herpes (HSV2) while in middle school.

Although HIV gets the most press, genital herpes is one of the most common sexually transmitted viruses in the United States. Take a look at the these facts:

- Genital herpes infections can cause painful and recurring sores, blisters, or ulcers in or on the genital organs.
- HSV outbreaks may show up anywhere on the body.
- Most people with herpes have no symptoms and are unaware of their infection.
- Herpes is for life.
- A person with herpes is more susceptible to other infections when exposed.
- Herpes sores heighten the risk of future infections of other diseases that can be more fatal, such as HIV, which leads to AIDS.

More than one in five Americans are currently infected with herpes simplex I (HSV1)—the nonsexual type that results in cold sores—and herpes simplex II (HSV2)—the type that is contracted through sexual contact. And there are an estimated one million new cases every year. But "with or without visible symptoms, the disease can be transmitted between sex partners," says the CDC.

> Most people with herpes are unaware of their infection.

What kind of impact will herpes have on Shaniqua's life? Let's assume she abstains from sexual activity throughout high school and even college. Maybe she'll graduate from Harvard and meet the man of her dreams. Her gift to him on their wedding night will be genital herpes. And they will both go to their graves with the disease.

And let's say Shaniqua and her husband have been married for seven years. He's a successful businessman and a loving husband. Then on one of his many business trips, he cheats on her.

He returns home but doesn't tell her right away about his affair. Because he has herpes, he's more apt to contract another STD from the other woman. And he'll give that new infection—that he doesn't realize he now has—to his bride.

So the one choice Shaniqua made in middle school will forever affect her future.

Hepatitis B (HBV)

Karyn

Karyn, an energetic 17-year-old, will never forget her 16th birthday. Some of her friends decided to give her a great present—a visit to a body-piercing salon. Ryan, her boyfriend then, took her out for pizza afterward. Later they parked at a romantic spot, and, "Well, we didn't have intercourse, but we did almost everything else," she told me. The next day she felt ugly and used. She told him she'd never do that again, and he broke up with her on the spot.

Six months later she was in a doctor's office with chronic stomach pain. That's when she found out it wasn't her stomach that was hurting. It was her liver. She had hepatitis B. She'll never know if she got it from a dirty needle at the body-piercing salon or from the "kissing" with Ryan.

Hepatitis B (HBV) isn't discussed very often as an STD, but it is dangerous.

- HBV attacks the liver and can cause cirrhosis, liver cancer, and even death.
- HBV is transmitted through bodily fluids: blood and blood products, semen and vaginal fluids, and saliva.
- It can also be contracted by sharing IV needles or through intercourse, kissing, or oral sex.
- With the popularity of tatoos and body piercings, HBV is now becoming more problematic.
- Roughly 120,000 of the 200,000 HBV infections that occur each year—mostly in young adults—are acquired through sexual transmission.

HIV

Laticia and Brandi

> Dear Mr. Herman, I found out about two years ago that my big sister Brandi has had HIV for around six years. It has not gone into AIDS yet, but lately her white blood cell count has been going

down. She lost her virginity at 15, dropped out of school during 10th grade, and was pregnant around 19. She is the reason I wish to remain abstinent. I do not want to put myself at risk of contracting a disease. It is very important to me to be a virgin when I get married. I just hope the man I marry made the same choice.

To Laticia in the Texas panhandle, so do I.

- The human immunodeficiency virus (HIV) causes a syndrome called acquired immunodeficiency syndrome, or AIDS.
- AIDS makes it difficult for the body to fight off infections.
- The body tries to defend itself against the virus, but it's unable to do so.
- The virus reproduces itself uniquely.
- People with HIV are contagious for life.
- There is some treatment for HIV symptoms, but there's no cure. It is fatal.
- Technically, no one really dies from HIV. They usually die from some other infection or cancer that the body couldn't destroy because of a weakened immune system.
- There are an estimated 50,000 new cases of HIV infections reported in the United States each year.
- Three years ago there were 800,000 AIDS cases in the United States.
- The average length of time between diagnosis and death is 10 to 29 years.
- It's the leading cause of death of people ages 25 to 44.

This is the virus that took the lives of Evon and Ashli, just because someone chose to lie about his sexual past when he donated blood.

HPV

Emily's Story

I met Emily when she was an eighth grader. She had long, curly, blonde hair, and her face was slightly swollen from crying. She talked to me after I spoke at her school.

"I just wanted to thank you for your message," she said. "Thank you for telling all my friends the truth. I've been sexually active. About six months ago I went to the doctor and discovered I have HPV. A couple of months back we discovered that I have the beginnings of cervical cancer. I've already had a colposcopy and a biopsy."

A courageous smile spread across her face. "It's not that I'm going to die. I just have to be careful and work with the doctors. . . . And I just wanted to thank you for warning my friends in time."

A colposcopy? I didn't even know what the procedure was, so why should this young teen have to know?

HPV is short for human papillomavirus. It's the fastest spreading STD, with 5.5 million new cases each year and an estimated 20 million people currently infected. That makes it the most common STD in our nation.

- HPV can cause genital warts, but most infected people don't have noticeable symptoms.
- There are approximately 100 different types of HPV.
- Over 30 of these types are sexually transmitted and cause genital HPV, which cannot be entirely prevented by a condom. This virus isn't limited to blood, semen, or mucus membranes. Any area around the anus, scrotum, penis, or vagina is highly contagious. A condom can't cover those areas.
- HPV can be transmitted with skin-to-skin contact by any part of the hands, genitals, face, or the body.
- The HPV virus is found in 99.7 percent of all cervical cancers. That makes HPV a more common killer of American women than AIDS.

Sadly, Emily was never told the truth. But now she knows. And she also knows the details of biopsy and colposcopy procedures. She may even get the chance to experience cancer treatment as well.

High-risk sexual activity: *any genital contact of any kind.* After making over 2,000 presentations in high schools, I've heard some frightening things. You've got to know that *any* genital contact is a sexual activity that can have serious effects.

> HPV is a more common killer of women than AIDS.

Other Infections

There are more infections passed through sexual contact than the ones we've discussed briefly in this chapter. And the list continues to grow. It's time for truth. Physicians and nurses are now discovering genital herpes lesions, gonorrhea, and genital warts in the *throat.* You can get HPV even in your mouth. Yes, oral sex is risky.

The Prevention and the Cure

Is there a way to prevent STDs? Of course! Abstinence before marriage and monogamy (being faithful to one person) in marriage.

Some of you may be saying, "It's too late—I've already blown it." So please listen closely. If you have been involved in sexual activity, get examined. There's no excuse not to. Step past your embarrassment and be honest and responsible. Doctors can treat and cure bacterial infections *if they know you are infected.* Ignorance is not bliss. So get examined *now*, before you have to suffer lifelong consequences you could have avoided.

The Myth of "Safe Sex"

If you're still reading this chapter, I applaud you! This stuff can be tough to read about.

Contraceptives are helpful for preventing unwanted pregnancies. But do they provide any protection against STDs?

Take a look for yourself.

Think You've Got It Covered?

Take this self-test to see if you're right . . .

| Birth control methods: withdrawal, condoms, birth control pills, Depo-Provera (injection), Norplant (implant), or abstinence | Protection against: pregnancy, HIV, HPV, or emotional scars |

You've heard about protection when it comes to "safe sex." Find out how safe you and your friends are by completing the questions below.

1. Of the above birth control methods, how do condoms rank in preventing pregnancy?

> First – 100% effective
> Second – 99% effective
> Third – 94% effective
> Fourth – 84% effective
> Last – 76% effective

2. Which of the birth control methods protects you from emotional scars?

> Withdrawal
> Condoms
> Birth control pills
> Abstinence

3. To prevent HIV transmission, are condoms more effective than all other birth control methods?

> Yes
> No

4. If the prevention rate for *pregnancy* is 76% when using the withdrawal method, what is the protection rate for *HIV* using the same method?

> 99%
> 42%
> 12%
> None

5. Of the six birth control methods listed, four offer *no* protection from HIV. Abstinence offers *complete* protection. Which remaining one offers only *limited* protection?

> Withdrawal
> Birth control pills
> Condom
> My dad's shotgun (just kidding!)

6. Is there any way to be safe from all these four possible consequences?

> No, so have sex anyway.
> Yes!

Answers

1. Fourth. Withdrawal is worse, but abstinence ranks at 100% protection!
2. Abstinence. None of the other three methods can protect your heart—if you have sexual experiences outside marriage, you will have emotional scars.
3. No. Condoms protect from HIV only 57% to 90% of the time, while abstinence protects 100% of the time.
4. None. HIV is transmittable during sexual exposure, even if withdrawal is used prior to ejaculation.
5. Condom. Condoms never eliminate the risk of contracting HIV. They only reduce the risk of infection.
6. It should be clear that abstinence until marriage should protect you from all the possible consequences listed above. Sure you can have sex. Great sex

and lots of it! Just not until you are married and you're both faithful to each other. And if you need to start over, get yourself examined, and practice abstinence from now on.

Contraceptives may be better than nothing, but they give false hope. They may provide risk *reduction*, but not risk *elimination*.

Even under the best circumstances, condoms do not offer complete protection. This doesn't account for factors like incorrect use, inconsistent use, condoms that break, non-covered areas, drug and alcohol abuse, or a hidden STD in a partner.

Do you really want to hang your future and your life on a condom or other birth control device for a few minutes of sex?

> **There's no such thing as "safe sex."**

There's no such thing as "safe sex."

Here's a simple rule to live by: Keep your clothes on. Don't cross the tan line! If the sun doesn't touch it, nobody else's son ought to be touchin' it either!

> *All of the risks you mentioned, all of the examples of what can happen, really got me thinking. A good moment right now isn't worth the risk of me contracting something that will ruin me in some way. However, I have had oral sex with my boyfriend, and a lot of touching type things, and I know you can contract diseases from these as well. In your opinion, do you think I should get checked out?*
>
> *—Simone, CA*

Thanks, Simone. And yes, I think you should get examined. Even if nothing comes from it, getting checked shows maturity. Could you be infected? Absolutely. And if you are, you deserve the help of a physician.

Your Final Chapter?

Will this chapter motivate you and your friends to change your dating and sexual habits? I hope so. You deserve life and not death. But you have to choose it. Here are some teens who already have:

I'm saving sex for marriage. No guy is worth losing my life over.

—*Crystal, TX*

I have never experienced sex and have always planned to wait until marriage. I am currently in a relationship of seven months. As we both sat together and listened to you, we decided that sex wasn't going to be something we would have to experience at such a young age.

—*Keena, TX*

I haven't always made the best decisions in the past, but today, after I heard your story, I decided to practice abstinence from now on. I say from now on because I'm not a virgin. But you said we could make the change whenever we want, and I want this to be a new beginning for me. It's my 18th birthday, and I think that's as good a time as any to begin my second chance. Sex is just not worth all the pain and the risk.

—*Linda, OH*

I'm going to take your advice. I think I will try and talk to my mom about getting checked out, and see what she says. I have been praying and talking to God about my situation, and it has helped. I have also decided to become a renewed virgin. I know now that it was wrong to have sex with this guy. All it did was cause problems. And now he is pretty much out of my life. I've discovered he never really cared about me. It means a lot to me to know that, as a parent, you would appreciate your child's decision to be responsible by going to see the doctor.

—*Tricia, IL*

It isn't fair that women bear the brunt of these STDs. Yes, men are at risk too. But because a woman's body is designed to be "receptive," it's much easier for her to get an infection. To put it bluntly, these diseases have much more drastic consequences for women than for men.

To the real men out there . . .

I'm going to challenge the guys reading this book. The women in your life are worth fighting for. If we are willing to cross the globe to defend our nation militarily, then we need to start by fighting for health right here at home. Listen to this comment I received recently:

> *You've challenged us. My three friends and I are enrolled to go into the Marines and Navy this fall. Yeah, we're going to begin defending our women right here. Just wanted to say thanks.*

—Mike, IN

Find Out More

If you've been involved in any sexual activity, tell your physician. Most know about these STDs, but some don't. Tell your doctor you want to be examined for bacterial and viral infections that can be transmitted by sexual exposure. If the doctor only gives you a condom and says, "Be safe," you haven't found the right doctor.

You can also contact:

National Physicians Center for Family Resources
402 Office Park Drive, Suite 307
Birmingham, Alabama 35223
877-870-1890
physicianscenter.org

If you haven't been involved in any sexual activity, great job! Keep going.

If I get a chance to speak to your future husband or wife, what do you want me to say? Probably the same thing they recently told me to say to you: "Start over for me."

It comes down to character.

What about you? Why not *begin* your story with respect and character? If you want a safe, faithful marriage, start working on that *before* you say "I do."

If I get a chance to speak to your future husband or wife, what do you want me to say? Probably the same thing they recently told me to say to you: "Start over for me."

twisted purposes
Abuse, Harassment, Rape

Actually, there are more consequences of not following God's plan for our sexuality.

When sin becomes acceptable in society, crime increases.

Like in cases of sexual abuse, sexual harassment, or rape. We'll talk about those in this chapter—and what you can do about it. But first I want you to meet someone very special.

Abuse

Chelsea's Story

When I was 13, I was molested by my stepfather. And when I was with him, he taught me that I was not worth anything and was only good to be walked over. So for the past five years of my life,

I had no self-respect. My mom would tell me that I am a good person and deserved to be treated with respect. But I did not believe her. I have a real trust problem with her, partly because I'm still mad at her 'cause she allowed this to go on right under her nose. It took her four years to finally get it that I was not lying . . . the other part is her telling me that it wasn't my stepfather's fault—that I "tempted" him to have sex with me somehow. So after that I've never really felt "clean." Since I'm dirty and used anyway now, I let guys use me because I thought that was the only way I could get a guy to like me. When you told your whole story I realized I was wrong. I didn't have to have sex with a guy just because my step-father had sex with me. I deserved a lot more than I was getting. I can't say it was a miracle and all of a sudden I have a lot of self-respect, but I am working a lot harder on it now. Since then, I have been approached by two different guys—both wanting the same thing. I told them I was not going to let myself be used as a toy. (I was so proud of myself!!!) Now I realize I deserve to be respected.

—Chelsea, NY

If Chelsea's story rings true for you, I want to say this to you:
It was not your fault.
You did nothing wrong.

The choice of abuse was made by a sick, perverted person. It was *his* or *her* choice to carry out such evil.

You are innocent.

It doesn't matter what you looked like, what you wore, what you said or didn't say, or what you did or didn't do. Anyone who acts in a sexual way toward a child or teen—whether fondling, caressing, going all the way, or practicing pornographic acts—is *wrong*. It's sin, and God condemns it. The Bible makes that very clear.

> You must never have sexual intercourse with a close rela-
> tive. . . . Do not have sexual intercourse with your sister or half
> sister. . . . Do not have sexual intercourse with your grand-

daughter. . . . Do not have sexual intercourse with both a woman and her daughter. (Leviticus 18:6, 9, 10, 17)

And . . .

If anyone causes one of these little ones who trusts in me to lose faith, it would be better for that person to be thrown into the sea with a large millstone tied around the neck. (Matthew 18:6)

But do you ever wonder where God was when you were abused? Was he out to lunch? Did he turn his head and let it go on? No. He was right there in that room with you when you were being abused, holding you in his arms. He was grieved and angry at the person who abused you. Someday God will make that abuser pay for what he has done to you. And God's vengeance will be much worse than anything you could think up.

Are you protecting someone else?

Maybe you think you had to have sex with a certain person to protect someone else. Check out this for-instance:

My friend finally decided to confide in me tonight. I'm guessing your speech made a real impact on her today. She told me some things that her mother's ex-boyfriend did to her that make her feel guilty. She blames herself for what happened, and I don't know what to tell her. I am trying to help her see that it wasn't her fault, because when these things happened she was only nine and there was nothing she could have done to stop it. She blames herself for letting this guy touch her, but she tells me that had she not done these things he said he'd have hurt her mother. I don't know what to tell her or what to do to help her. I am searching for God's answers, but sometimes it is hard to know where to look.

—Wendy, IL

If you let him, God will heal your heart and help you regain the self-respect that you and other Chelseas feel you lost.

It was *not* your fault.

The abuse wasn't your
fault. You did
nothing wrong.

Can guys be abused?

Sexual abuse isn't limited to girls. It can happen to guys too. Just ask Dave. When he was eight, an older girl cousin who baby-sat him raped him and then locked him in the closet. And Walt's stepfather repeatedly had sex with him.

If you are a guy reading this and you've been abused, you're not alone. And it's not your fault, either. If you were abused by a woman, it doesn't mean that you're weak or that you're less of a man. If you were abused by a man, it doesn't mean that you're gay or that you have gay tendencies or that the man saw something gay in you.

These pedophiles—sexual abusers of children—may have targeted you, but it's not because of anything you've done or who you are. Simply put, they were corrupted by Twisted's evil.

If you were abused by
a man, it doesn't mean
that man saw
something gay in you.

Abuse strikes deeply at the heart and soul of anyone—guy or girl—who has been in that situation. It makes them feel dirty and used. But for a male, abuse attacks his manhood, triggering a deep guilt and a sense that he'll never be a true man if he "let" someone use him that way.

That again is Twisted's influence creeping in. Do not allow him to sink his fangs into your heart or mind.

God sees you and calls you clean. He wants to comfort you and help you recover. He wants to help you get rid of all the feelings and thoughts that haunt you. And he will rebuild you on the inside. God is a true Father you can trust.

Healing from Abuse

A girl named Wanda gave me this note a couple of years ago:

> I'm a sophomore. When I heard we were going to have another speaker I just thought, Oh, great. But you got to me. See, when I was growing up, my grandpa sexually abused me. Our family hasn't been the same since he went to jail. And the worst part was, he died in there. We hadn't seen him for almost six years.
>
> —Wanda, Alberta, Canada

There's no question that abuse causes deep inner scars that can take years to heal. In talking to Wanda, it was obvious to me that somehow she had found a way to forgive and love her grandfather in spite of what he had done to her. The result was a healed heart.

You can have that healing too. It all starts here.

#1: Admit to yourself that you've been abused.

Realize that what happened to you is wrong and evil. It was not God's plan for that person to abuse you. But when people choose to do wrong, others suffer for it. You are not wrong or evil. What happened was *not* your fault.

#2: Tell someone you trust.

It may be a parent, a teacher, a youth group leader, or the police. But tell someone. Do it right away. If that person doesn't believe you, find someone who does.

That's what a girl named Marian had to do. She had told a teacher that her uncle had abused her and her sisters, but the teacher didn't believe her. The teacher phoned her uncle, who was her guardian while her parents were on a trip. When the uncle threatened her life and her sisters' lives, Marian decided they had suffered enough. So she walked to the local police station at 2 a.m., after her uncle had sexually abused her again. Because the evidence was still there in her bed at 3 a.m. when the police showed up at the door, the uncle was arrested immediately.

Telling someone takes huge courage. But that abuser must be stopped before they hurt you again—or someone else.

Forgive them? Are you crazy?

If you've been abused, forgiving may be the last thing on your mind. I can't blame you. What happened to you is painful and evil, and it would be very hard not to hate and fear the one who abused you.

> Forgiveness doesn't mean you become a doormat.

So let's be clear about what forgiveness is and what it is not. Choosing to forgive means you release yourself from the cycle of hate, guilt, anger, fear, and bitterness. You're no longer letting the person who abused you control your life. But it doesn't mean you become a doormat. You're not letting the abuser off the hook either.

If this person is someone you have to be around (a parent, step-parent, or relative who lives with you), go out of your way to make sure you won't be home alone with that person, even if he or she has apologized. If the person is truly sorry, then he will be *repentant*, which means apologizing to you, changing his actions, and getting help on his own—without being forced to by a court's order—to hold him accountable for his actions.

Statistics have shown that it's very difficult for pedophiles to be reformed. So don't allow yourself to be pulled in by any mind games. If the person approaches you again, tell a trusted adult immediately.

Harassment: Too Close for Comfort

When I was a youth minister several years ago, there was a particularly beautiful girl in my youth group. Everywhere we went as a group, the heads of men—old and young alike—would turn when she walked into a room. Even her shyness added to her mystique. But she was rarely asked out on a date, and when she was, it was only by the rude guys whose courage was laced with brazen disregard. All the quality young men were too awed by her beauty to ask her out. That was when I really began my quest to help develop confident, quality young men who could see past "pretty" to the real person. (We'll talk more about this later.)

If you are reading this and you too have a physical body that gets comments and whistles, you'll be able to relate. I've met many teens who find their attractiveness to be a curse. They get looks and attention they don't want. Sometimes these actions can cut deeply.

Here's an example. Rachel is a high school freshman. Recently a teacher at her school was caught—on videotape—ogling her body in a very unsettling way. He was confronted by her parents and school officials, but her parents were told nothing else could be done. Rachel has had a hard time dealing with her physical beauty ever since. I have tried over and over again to let her see that she's beautiful for who she is inside, but she's much more aware of the stares and looks that men give her.

Here's another teen's story:

Everyone knew he was a strange teacher. But we just kinda blew him off, ya know? He was about 30 years old, single, fairly cool at times, and was the cross-country coach. But when he always hung around me and some of my friends, it began to make me feel uncomfortable. He'd look over my shoulder at my paperwork and begin giving me a shoulder rub or back rub. He always complimented me on my looks and how fortunate the guys were to be able to ask me out. He also would talk about my younger sister and her body, how sexy she was. It was rumored that he was dating a senior girl at the time. The following year after she had graduated, the rumor was verified. Now that she's 18, he was "out of trouble" and wasn't afraid to say that they hooked up all the time. I'll never forget when he grabbed a girl's black high-heeled shoe sitting on the stereo speaker by his desk and in front of the class said, "Oh, the trouble I'd get into if I told you the things I did with the person who fits this shoe."

—*Kelle, MI*

This behavior doesn't stop with the girls. Another coach once tore into the character of a handsome boy who was the high school quarterback. "Why are you so uptight?" the coach asked. "You just need to chill out. What you need is to get laid. Look, I'll give you Jamie, the trainer. She wants you and is here for you. Take her!"

I don't believe we should be running around yelling "Sexual harassment!" at every turn. But there are some cases where you need to have someone defend you.

What is sexual harassment?

If someone makes any comments or actions that you did not ask for, that you do not want, and that are of a sexual nature, that's sexual harassment. It doesn't matter whether the person is your age, younger, or older. (For detailed information, visit PureRevolution.com.)

What do you do if you are being harassed? Even if the person is in a position of authority over you, you need to take action. Follow the steps below.

#1: Tell the person, "Stop. I don't like that."
Even better, be specific about what offends you. "Do not rub my back every time you pass by." "I hate the comments you make about my chest. They are not appropriate."

#2: If it continues, tell the person the consequences.
Say something like this: "I don't like those comments, those actions, or being touched that way. If you don't stop, I'll report you." Giving a consequence is often enough to stop the person in his tracks.

Take action! Don't put up with sexual harassment.

#3: If the person says, "Aw, come on! I was just teasing. Can't you take a joke?" tell them it wasn't funny to you.

Don't fall for this line. Tell them you'll report them if they don't stop teasing.

#4: If the teasing, language, or actions persist, report the harassment.
Tell a person in authority where the harassment is happening, and also tell your parents or guardians. Contact a lawyer if you have a valid reason to contact them for their services. Then you can explain to your harasser's parent, supervisor, or other authority that you've contacted legal counsel to find out whether you have a case.

The goal isn't to create a lot of unneeded lawsuits. But don't put up with sexual harassment. Because the people in the stories above did not file charges, these coaches and teachers are still in classes today, probably harassing other teens.

Like sexual abuse, sexual harassment is not your fault. You've done nothing wrong.

The Horror of Rape

In my talks at high schools, I describe the following scenario (told to me by Pam Stenzel, whom I wrote about earlier) to find out how girls feel about rape. I ask this question:

"Girls, I have two scenarios that I want you to pick from: A or B. There is no other option. Here's scenario A. Let's say you are at the mall, and you return to the parking lot alone to get your purse. Just as you reach your car, a van pulls up. Two guys get out of the van and begin to knife you repeatedly. Then, when they see somebody coming, they jump back into the van and speed away. The other person sees you and takes you to the hospital. You'll survive, but it hurts.

"Now, scenario B. You are at the same mall, same parking lot, same car. A van pulls up. Two guys get out of the van. This time they don't stab you. Instead they throw you into the van and take you to a remote area, where they rape you repeatedly. They bring you back to your car and throw you on the ground. Again someone comes and they speed away. This person takes you to the hospital. You'll survive, but it hurts.

"Girls, these are two ugly scenarios. But if you had to choose A or B, which would you pick?"

Do you know what every American and Australian high school girl I've asked has chosen? Scenario A. Loudly!

This may seem like an extreme example, but the fact that girls would rather be knifed repeatedly than raped tells me a couple of things. First, that girls see sex as an intimate act. Second, that sex is not just a physical act.

Date rape: Is a no really a yes?

I've met many young men who ask in all sincerity, "When she says no, does she really mean yes? At least that she wants me to keep trying?" Others have said, "We all know that saying no is just a way to get out of the responsibility. She wants it as bad as I do, but if she says no, then she can try to pin date rape on me later."

> Sex is not just a physical act.

No girl ever wants someone to steal something from her that is so personal, so private, so much a part of her, as her virginity. Women know better than most men the vulnerability of a woman's sexuality. They realize the physical difference between the sexes. They want to be an equal partner with equal respect and equal control. And that is well deserved.

The rules are pretty simple, I think. Yes means yes, and no means "Get your ugly, selfish, lust-driven hands off me before I head-butt your nose, poke you in the eyes, and crush your groin!" (That's for my daughter, Brianna.)

So, guys, take your hands off your dates. And girls, please say no far earlier than 20 minutes into a heated kissing round in some secluded location. Date rape happens too often not because the girl "changed her mind," but because she is unaware of how early sexual arousal occurs for the male or because he may think her no means "Go ahead, convince me" or "Let's make it rough."

Dream On

Every week I meet teens who have a lot of pain in their lives because of choices other people have made.

What would the world be like if young men

- fought for purity and honor?
- refused to brag in the locker room about Friday's conquest?
- had the courage to keep their commitments even when things got tough?
- stood for what is right and refused to do anything to harm either themselves or those they love?

What would the world be like if young women

- were not intimidated by men, or by women who are more beautiful or successful, because their inner beauty and character shapes their identity?
- didn't compete for love and attention, and knew how to love and nurture others?

- could fully bond in marriage someday because there's no previous sexual history?
- took a stand against violence and harassment?

Maybe you're wondering, *Could that really happen, for me?* Yes! You *can* have a world like that, and incredible relationships. But you've got to refuse to give in to Twisted's thinking.

Like teens all around the country, *you* can certainly live these dreams. And you can launch a new revolution—a pure revolution!

guys talk . . .

About Girls, How They Dress, and Sexy Thoughts

Amazing how many of you girls raced to this section, even though it's for guys.

In the many guy retreats and camps I've been part of, I've had some mind-blowing conversations. The questions have been very honest and real.

So let's talk about some important stuff, like how girls dress, controlling your mind, and the "M" word.

We shouldn't blame girls for our own thoughts. But what's the solution when girls dress so provocatively that it's hard *not* to have sexual thoughts?

Girls, since you're reading this I'm including you too.

God has created us guys to be aroused visually. A beautiful girl is naturally attractive to us for a reason; to excite us and help us to reproduce. But we're different than animals. We have self-control and discernment. Arousal doesn't mean "turn off your mind."

You see, God wants the sexual experience to be exciting for a husband and wife—and filled with passion and love. God *wants* you to be turned on . . . that's natural. But he sets boundaries: such physical expression should be only with your wife. No one else. *Period*. No "But I think I'm in love." No "But everybody else is having sex." God is clear—no one but a husband and wife should engage in sexual activity.

However, because Twisted has made his mark, sexual activity outside of marriage can cause arousal too. Understanding that, women need to be very careful about how they dress. A woman's appearance has incredible power over a guy. And she needs to choose not to abuse that power.

Girls, please realize that we think you are absolutely stunning. But you must try to be modest when it comes to clothing. We are *trying* to develop self-control and self-discipline, but having you parade around wearing a thong bikini is a bit much. That kind of stimulation causes a very natural process to kick in.

A Guy's Sexual System

For guys, there's a point of sexual excitement that makes stopping difficult. A lot of girls might assume a guy gets sexually aroused in the same way and at the same time as she does. Not at all. We men are aroused *much earlier* than women, and testosterone races through our bodies, giving us a rush of strength and excitement. God created this drive to not stop. Why? Because it was only to be initiated in marriage, where you don't have to stop.

> For guys, there's a point of sexual excitement that makes stopping difficult.

So girls, don't be fooled into thinking you can have an extended make-out session and maybe some caressing or more and then tell him no. Many guys won't stop there since they've been turned on long before and don't choose to stop until their sex drive fulfills itself.

It's All about Life

Guys, isn't it interesting how we are attracted to areas of a woman's body that God created for nurture and life? The breasts, the pelvic region, the lower abdomen—these are all made by God to give life. Why are we particularly interested in them? Because sex is about life. It's the expression of intimate life in a marriage between two people. And it creates new life.

Are we drawn to features of strength—like a strong face, broad shoulders, a thick chest, and a lean torso—like women are to men? No. We're drawn to breasts, belly buttons, and backsides! Ladies, that's why you need to be very careful about using those parts of your body to draw men to you. We're already naturally drawn, just because of the way God made us. We don't need any help in that department.

Does this mean that guys can't do anything about their own "looking"? Sorry guys, we're not off the hook. To *lust* is to want someone sexually who is not your spouse. It's wrong to lust, even if a girl tempts you. Jesus made that clear: "I say, anyone who even looks at a woman with lust in his eye has already committed adultery with her in his heart." So you guys are responsible for your thoughts and actions too.

> We guys are naturally drawn to you girls. We don't need any help in that department.

You don't want girls walking around in oversized gunnysacks, right? We men have to take the lead here. We have to be true men, true protectors of women, as God has created us to be. How can we do that?

We need to realize that being drawn to a woman's body is natural and God-given. There's nothing wrong with admiring the beauty of a woman. It's when that admiration becomes twisted—when we start thinking about sex with a woman who isn't our wife—that it becomes wrong.

So we need to learn how to control our mind. We're men, not animals, right? It's time we act like men of honor and strength.

Mind Control—You Can Do It

The remote control: a tool we men are familiar with. It's a lot like how we function. We love to be in control, which is why not being able to control our mind freaks us out. Let's use this to our mental advantage.

When you're hanging out with the guys at the mall and that gorgeous girl walks by, what happens? You start to heat up. *She sure is hot,* you think. And what's the next step? *I'd love to go out with her. Get to know her. I mean, really get to know her . . .*

So what can you do to stop this natural progression that's only for marriage?

Change the Channel

Before your mind races into a skin scene, change the channel. Turn your head and look somewhere else. Pray. Thank God for his creativity in making such a beautiful woman. Ask him for strength to be pure.

But don't linger and stare. If you continue staring, you'll naturally undress her in your mind. And when you do that you've not only crossed the line of respect and honor, you've also sinned. So focus on a new picture. Call Jesus' name in a quick prayer for strength.

When we were discussing this at a youth event in Atlanta, guys began asking questions about the remote-control idea. One honest guy said, "But what do you do when they're on *every* channel?" We laughed, but we knew he had a point.

Do you want to know what to do? Let's do a test to see if my idea works.

Go ahead and picture yourself at the beach or swimming pool. You're there having a great time. You're totally surrounded by God's workmanship—beautiful women. You've been changing the channel, but on every station in your brain you see a skimpy suit clinging to curves. What should you do?

Picture your grandma.

Aha! It worked, didn't it? I saw you jumping out of your chair as the two pictures clashed in your mind. Never would you sexualize an image of your grandparent. So think of Grandma when your mind freezes on the female channel.

Above all, find *some* way to control your thoughts. You must master your thought life. There is no compromising. If you cannot do it alone, get help and support from an older mentor or a pastor.

You might also begin a fast. Forcing your hunger drive under control can help you focus more on spiritual nutrition. Get medical guidance from a doctor if you are going to fast, though.

Together, mind control and fasting can empower you to keep your thoughts in check. If you have extreme trouble or have had exposure to pornography, you may need counseling. Sometimes sexual addictions can be so deeply entrenched in your mind that you need professional help to think clearly again. But you can do it—you have the strength and the courage to do it. Now is the time to master your urges. Sexual activity is not play, and neither is sexual thinking. Don't hand Twisted the tools for destroying your life.

Your habits now are shaping you into the kind of husband you'll be someday. Be the kind of man every woman would want. Women are looking for guys who can control their minds.

> Sexual activity is not play. And neither is sexual thinking.

When you get married you'll still see beautiful women all the time—often women who are more physically attractive than your wife. But when you see those women, will your wife see you drool all over yourself? Or will she see her faithful and strong husband appreciate beauty as God created men to do and then look the other way?

The "M" Word

Deep breath here. Since we're talking about controlling the mind, let's address the topic of masturbation.

Yeah, sure it's a physical action. But it also requires the mind's involvement. Physically, you cannot get a girl pregnant that way. You cannot get an STD from someone else if you are alone. And, contrary to myth, you won't grow hair in strange places.

The most common questions about masturbation are:

- Is it a sin or not?
- Can it hurt you or not?

Let me cut to the chase. Masturbation can only occur if you have thoughts of lust in your mind. As we read earlier, Jesus tells us not to lust or have impure thoughts.

Masturbation is unhealthy for both spiritual and psychological reasons. When you ejaculate, enkephalins and endorphins are released in your mind, giving you a good feeling. Yes, God planned this so that sex would feel mind-boggling. This also causes a bonding experience in your mind with the person you're focusing on during ejaculation or climax. Again, this is God's plan, so that when you are married you will continually bond psychologically to your spouse. Very cool. As you age, the physical body and sexual experiences may change, but there's a powerful connection between you and your spouse, already developed over the years.

Ejaculating, or climaxing, while *not* focusing on your spouse causes you to bond to whatever image (real or not) you do focus on. This continual bonding with anyone or anything other than your spouse will cause problems in the future. When you do get married, those past images will flash through your mind when you have sex with your wife.

If a man has to close his eyes and picture someone other than his wife to climax, is he really making love to her? Would you have a problem if your wife imagined other men while she's having sex with you? Thought so.

The Bible doesn't specifically say that masturbation is wrong. But if you read carefully, you'll know God's position on the question. Your seed (semen) was created for the purpose of conception. The sexual experience is to be with your spouse only. So don't give in to Twisted, who is trying to trap you.

Masturbation is neither godly nor honorable. And as I mentioned earlier, sex has always been about life or death. You can develop the strength of self-control. You don't have to masturbate. So choose life.

Feeling a Little Guilty?

What guy hasn't felt some guilt over a little too much "looking" at a woman? Or the struggle with the "M" word?

Hey guys, if you are perfect, your name would sound a lot like Jesus! I'm not saying it's okay to sin or do whatever you want. But knowing that you're a sinner, saved by grace, should help you deal with the guilt that accumulates on your soul when you fail.

Simply confess your sins when you fall into Twisted's trap, reconnect with someone who will encourage and mentor you, and work on developing your self-control. Cleansing your mind of sexual thoughts will help too! So cut out the diet of sex-laden music and read more of God's Word. Try what the apostle Paul (who never married, and since he's a guy, most likely had to deal with these struggles throughout his lifetime) suggests: "Fix your thoughts on what is true and honorable and right. Think about things that are pure and lovely and admirable. Think about things that are excellent and worthy of praise."

Clean thoughts. Bringing your mind under control will help you win this battle. It may seem like a small thing today, but it can help you avoid what has become an addiction for many men.

10

girls dish . . .

About Guys, Beauty, and What They Really Want out of Sex

Since a guy can't do "girl talk," I asked girls in high school and college what they thought. Here's what they had to say.

Brittlee, a young woman who works with young teen girls, explained to me what she's learned in her experiences concerning the clothes girls wear: "Girls usually don't understand how much the way they dress affects guys. When girls dress scandalously, men are attracted, and they lust over what they see."

Aimee agrees. She spends her time directing and coaching a teen dance troupe called Breakdown, which promotes sexual purity. Here are her thoughts:

What you wear
determines the kind of
guy you attract.

If you're like me, you have to admit that it's nice to get noticed every once in a while. Part of every woman longs for attention. After all, that's what makeup, hair spray, jewelry, and great shoes were invented for (not to mention the Wonderbra)! Of course we want to get the attention of guys. But let's face it—we also want other girls to look at us. It's the nature of a woman. But why?

We want to look cute, pretty, or fashionable because we want to be liked. For some of us this stems from an inherent insecurity in not feeling adequate in our own, plain selves. Others never really outgrow the "playing dress-up" mentality because, well . . . it's fun! There's nothing wrong with wanting to look nice, but I've realized that the type of clothes I choose to wear determines what kind of man I attract. Let me give you an example.

A while back I attended an evening church service wearing some pants that were a little on the tight side. . . . After the service a man followed me to my car and proceeded to [talk to me] as he continued to look me up and down. I felt like a sexual object. His intentions were clear. . . . I finally got in my car and drove away, feeling dirty and violated. I knew without a shadow of a doubt that my outfit had sent the wrong message about the kind of person I was. I felt guilty, shamed, and most importantly, partly responsible for his behavior. Needless to say, I've never worn *those* pants again.

Attract the kind of guy you want.

Here's Brittlee's advice: "Be attracted to the kind of guy you can see yourself serious with down the road. The kind of guy you'd want to be married to. Dressing immodestly often attracts the wrong kind of guy."

Consider this e-mail from 16-year-old Audra:

After the assembly you gave I was talking to some guys about what you had gone over with us and one of them said (the rest agreed),

"Well, all he did was make it harder for the guys to get play." I was so mad at him. Of course I said something to him, but it seemed as though he didn't even care. I don't get it. I thought he was a really, really great and caring guy.

Aimee is bluntly honest: "When a woman dresses 'sexy,' she will attract a man who only wants sex—not a real relationship. Likewise, when a woman dresses modestly, she should attract a man who is interested in more than just her body. If you've had a chance to read the 'Guys Talk' chapter, then you know how guys struggle with sexual thoughts. As women we can choose to help guys out by being careful of what we wear. If you want a guy who's interested in you for your mind, heart, and soul, you won't attract him by wearing bootie shorts and a halter top. Besides . . . who really looks good in that?!"

Accountability between friends is very important when it comes to dressing modestly. Sometimes what a friend sees and what you think about what you are wearing can be very different. "A girl can still dress in the fads," continues Brittlee, "but she needs to do it tastefully, reflecting her calling to be a woman who professes to worship God."

> Guard your heart. Don't give it away easily.

Girls want friendships and emotional connections. Because of that, it's especially important for girls to guard their hearts in a relationship. Don't give it away easily or you will regret it later.

When you're dating someone, it's easy to get attached quickly and to start thinking about the future. "Even after a first date, we tend to want to start planning our wedding and the names of our children," Brittlee explains. "Guarding your heart means guarding your personality and mind, not confusing yourself with thoughts that are not meant to be until later on in life, when marriage is a real possibility."

Girls' hearts tend to get attached easily, dragging their thoughts and emotions along for the ride. That's very dangerous! Sometimes the ride stops abruptly, and the debris left from the crash takes a long time to clean up. Train your mind to think clearly and not daydream about a future with that guy who seems so perfect. Don't waste your emotions on someone you aren't going to spend your life with.

It's all part of a girl's life.

Here's a fact from Marilyn Morris, president of Aim for Success, Inc., that guys and girls need to know:

> A woman is only fertile when she ovulates. Usually, this is also when she is most easily aroused sexually. Teenage girls and many women often have irregular cycles and are unable to tell when they are fertile. Because of this unpredictable cycle and not knowing exactly when she might ovulate, a girl needs to realize she might become pregnant almost any time she has sexual intercourse.

Why is this information so important for both girls and guys? Because when you're feeling the most "hot" is when you're the most likely to get pregnant. In other words, when you feel like you just can't say no is exactly when you *should* say no.

A great guy will never push you to give what God never intends you to give while you're single.

> A girl can become pregnant almost any time she has sex.

So where are all the great guys?

Good question!

After speaking at over 2,000 schools and youth retreats in the past 13 years, I've had so many young ladies come up to me afterward and ask, "Mr. Herman, where are all the great guys? They're certainly not in our school!"

Why are girls in America and Australia continually asking me this question?

Girls, the guys you want are those who have a depth of character. And there are many, many guys out there just like that. Guys who are strong, faithful, and godly and who won't cheat on you or use you.

I've met many of them. And many of them are reading this book. (Check out PureRevolution.com for more info.) So I'd like to share something with you girls. Contrary to what's advertised, a great guy is not defined by his athletic ability, his popularity, or his rock-hard abs.

I've met top-notch men who are in wheelchairs and use crutches, and others whose physical abilities are hampered for whatever reason. You may have a vision of what your dream hunk looks like, but don't underestimate guys like the ones I've met. A man who has taken time to develop his personality, his mind, and his inner strength has a lot more to offer than the guy whose greatest assets are his bulging biceps.

I can't even count the number of young men who develop late and don't fully mature until college—men who worked harder on their spirit and personality in high school than on their physique and public image. There are incredible guys who are still in the process of developing physically. And chances are, you haven't even given them a second look.

Take Jeff, a guy who was never considered "datable material" in high school because even as a senior, he was only four feet eleven and 81 pounds. Even more embarrassing, he had to sit on a built-up seat cushion to see over the dashboard of his car. He didn't start growing until he was a sophomore in college, when he grew six inches in one summer. Today he's five feet eleven. Recently he went to his high school reunion and shocked his classmates. They didn't even recognize him. The girls who'd turned him down for dates suddenly tried to get his attention because he was really handsome. He just smiled at them kindly and put his arm around his wife.

Now, all this is not to short-sheet the guys who are attractive and athletic. But I'm begging you girls not to be shallow. Try to see guys through God's eyes. If you do, you'll see some phenomenal men.

To find those guys you've got to be patient and friendly. You have to keep your standards high and your priorities straight. Trust that God will connect your paths in his perfect time. It will be worth the wait!

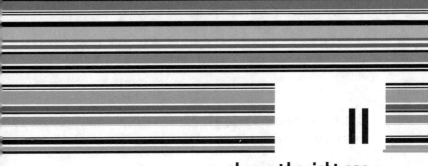

choose the right one
Be the Right One

Not every match is made in heaven. Make sure yours will be.

If you think about married couples you know, you probably think some of those marriages are working better than others. Not everyone waits for God to bring them his choice of a spouse. Many people settle. And many people regret it.

You are at a great time of life. Sure, you already may have some mistakes in your past. But choosing your spouse is most likely a choice you haven't made yet. How will you know you won't make a mistake?

You've got to ask God to prepare you for that person and help you recognize "the one."

Long ago in the Garden of Eden, God gave Adam and Eve to each other, and he's been matching men and women up ever since. Too much is at stake to pick your partner without his help.

Have you ever wondered why a guy or girl would date someone who's just not right for them?

Some couples are obviously meant for each other, while others . . . well, they're a different story.

For fun, let's do a short self-test. There's one for the girls and a different one for the guys. This isn't an exact science, but it can give you a good idea about whether *you* are what great guys and girls are looking for. Consider this a reality check with the spotlight on you!

Just mark the number of your answer in the space on the right. Then total the numbers to see your score. Be honest. There's no report card here.

Girls: Are you what he's looking for?
Take this SELF-TEST and see what guys think.

QUESTION

Do you complete your responsibilities daily?

ANSWER   SCORE

No. – 1   _____

Sometimes. – 3

Yes. – 5

QUESTION

Do you take care of yourself daily, including exercising regularly?

ANSWER   SCORE

No. – 1   _____

Sometimes. – 3

Yes. – 5

QUESTION

Do you like to dress attractively for a date?

ANSWER   **SCORE**

Never. How I look means nothing. – 1   ——

Sometimes. – 3

Always. I want to look great for him. – 5

QUESTION

What is your typical meal?

ANSWER   **SCORE**

Fast food. – 1   ——

Salad and soup. – 3

Full meal with my family. – 5

QUESTION

How many times a day do you brush your teeth?

ANSWER   **SCORE**

Once or less. – 1   ——

Twice. – 3

Three times or more. – 5

QUESTION

What would you do if you received $1,000?

ANSWER   **SCORE**

Go shopping. – 1   ——

Invest it. – 3

Take it to a shelter for the homeless. – 5

QUESTION

When you look in the mirror, do you like what you see?

ANSWER   **SCORE**

Not really. – 1   ——

It's getting better. – 3

Absolutely. – 5

QUESTION

Do you share *everything* with your close friends?

ANSWER   SCORE

Every day. – 1

Pretty much. – 3   ____

Not everything. – 5

QUESTION

Do guys say you talk too much?

ANSWER   SCORE

Yes, but they're guys! – 1

No. Too little actually. – 3   ____

Only after three mochas. – 5

QUESTION

How many children do you want to have?

ANSWER   SCORE

Yikes! None, thanks. – 1

At least eight! – 3   ____

A few, I think. – 5

QUESTION

Have you ever flirted with another guy when you're dating someone else?

ANSWER   SCORE

Of course. Who hasn't? – 1

Only a couple of times. – 3   ____

Never. That's wrong. – 5

QUESTION

Do you have a specific idea of what you want to do after graduation?

ANSWER	SCORE
Nope! – 1	___
Can't decide between a few choices. – 3	
Absolutely! – 5	

QUESTION

Do you feel like a relationship with a guy "completes" you?

ANSWER	SCORE
Yes. – 1	___
Kinda. – 3	
No. – 5	

QUESTION

At what level do you respect men in general?

ANSWER	SCORE
Low. – 1	___
Medium. – 3	
High. – 5	

QUESTION

How often do you laugh each day?

ANSWER	SCORE
Never. The world stinks. – 1	___
Depends on who I'm with. – 3	
Several times! – 5	

QUESTION

When you embarrass yourself, what do you do?

ANSWER	SCORE
I cry. – 1	___
I hide. – 3	
I laugh. – 5	

QUESTION

While you are with your boyfriend, the kissing goes on too long, and he wants you to have sex with him. You've pledged to be abstinent. What would you do?

ANSWER   SCORE

Do the horizontal mambo. – 1   ____

Compromise and only do some things to make him happy. – 3

Tell him that I respect him too much to compromise my standards. – 5

QUESTION

What would you prefer to do on a Saturday?

ANSWER   SCORE

Sit at home and be alone. – 1   ____

Take a walk with a friend. – 3

Hang out with my friends. – 5

QUESTION

How easy is it for you to spend time with guys?

ANSWER   SCORE

Not at all! – 1   ____

I can hang with most guys. – 3

I have friends who are guys. – 5

QUESTION

If you had to choose, would you pick a cute guy whose character isn't too good on the chance he'll change internally or an average-looking guy with great character on the chance he'll change physically?

ANSWER   SCORE

Take my chances on the cute guy. – 1   ____

Neither! I want both. – 3

Take my chances on the average-looking guy. – 5

QUESTION

If the most popular guy in school wanted to date you, but he touched you inappropriately, what would you do?

ANSWER	SCORE
I'd accept it. –1	—
I'd be embarrassed and freeze. – 3
I'd slap him silly. – 5

QUESTION

If there was an unpopular "geek" at school who was a very nice person, would you spend time with him or date him?

ANSWER	SCORE
Never. – 1	—
Spend time but not date. – 3
Yes, if we liked each other. – 5

QUESTION

How often do you pray and read your Bible?

ANSWER	SCORE
Never. – 1	—
Only at church. – 3
Several times a week. – 5

QUESTION

When you walk across the gym floor during a game, what are you most worried about?

ANSWER	SCORE
How I look. – 1	—
That I won't disturb the game. – 3
I don't usually worry much. – 5

QUESTION

If you are on a diet and someone offers you dessert that is way beyond the diet's rules, what would you do?

Eat it. I'm not hung up about rules. – 1

Only take a bite or eat a small portion. – 3

Kindly refuse. I'm strict on myself. – 5

TOTAL SCORE

In 20 years of youth ministry, I've found the following generalizations about each scoring category to be true. And remember, there's no "bad catch" in my opinion, no matter where you are in the scoring categories.

25–57 You've got a lot of potential. As you keep working on character issues, you may find more guys becoming more interested.

58–91 You've got a solid start. It may help to have an adult mentor you and help shape your beauty from the inside out. Keep going!

92–125 Wow! You are amazing. If he hasn't nabbed you yet, be patient. You're a great catch! Continue to work on those lower scores to be your best *you*.

Okay guys, some of you read through that test and you want the girls you know to take it, right? It'd be interesting to see their scores. But I've got one for you too.

Guys: Hot or Not?

Take this SELF-TEST and see what girls are looking for.

QUESTION

Who would you rather be?

ANSWER   SCORE

Million-dollar gambler. – 1

Firefighter. – 3

Volunteer in the Peace Corps. – 5

QUESTION

At what level do you respect women in general?

ANSWER

SCORE

Low. – 1

Medium. – 3

High. – 5

_____

QUESTION

If you had to choose, would you pick a sexy girl whose character isn't too good on the chance she'll change internally or an average-looking girl with great character on the chance she'll change physically?

ANSWER

SCORE

Take my chances on the cute girl.– 1

Neither! I want both. – 3

Take my chances on the average-looking girl. – 5

_____

QUESTION

When you meet a girl who looks great, what's the first thing you say?

ANSWER

SCORE

"Ugh! Me, man!" – 1

"You look good." – 3

"Your hair looks beautiful today," or something specific like that. – 5

_____

QUESTION

Which of these ideas is best for a great date?

ANSWER

SCORE

Just go hang out. – 1

Dinner and a movie. – 3

A picnic with food I prepared myself (yikes, I know!) and a long walk that ends near some flowers where I've already placed a card for her. – 5

_____

How often do you laugh each day?

Never. The world stinks. – 1
Depends on who I'm with. – 3
Several times! – 5

When you embarrass yourself, what do you do?

I cry. – 1
I hide. – 3
I laugh. – 5

How often do you pray and read your Bible?

Never. – 1
Only at church. – 3
Several times a week. – 5

Do you have a specific idea of what you want to do after graduation?

Nope! – 1
Can't decide between a few choices. – 3
Absolutely! – 5

Do you have specific plans in place to accomplish your goals?

What are goals? – 1
Too unclear yet. – 3
Yes, I do. – 5

QUESTION

How many children do you want to have?

ANSWER	SCORE
Yikes! None, thanks. – 1	_____
At least ten. I love chaos! – 3	
A few, I think. – 5	

QUESTION

When you hear the word *father*, what comes to your mind first?

ANSWER	SCORE
Carelessly absent. – 1	_____
Hardworking. – 3	
Honorable. – 5	

QUESTION

When you sit at a table with several forks on the left side of your plate, which one do you eat with first?

ANSWER	SCORE
I use my hands. – 1	_____
The one on the inside. – 3	
The one on the outside. – 5	

QUESTION

Have you ever enjoyed a huge water fight or massive shaving cream fight?

ANSWER	SCORE
Indubitably not. – 1	_____
Back when I was younger. – 3	
Yeah! Shoulda seen it! – 5	

QUESTION

Which of the following actors *most closely* represents how you carry yourself?

An Adam Sandler comedian type. – 1   _____

Pierce Brosnan as James Bond. – 3

Mel Gibson in *Braveheart*. – 5

QUESTION

At the end of a date, which phrase is *most similar* to how you'd conclude your date?

ANSWER   SCORE

"Catch ya later." – 1   _____

"I had a great time." – 3

"The only way to make this night more perfect is to know I can see you again." – 5

QUESTION

If you're out with your friends and you're the only one without a girlfriend, how do you feel?

ANSWER   SCORE

Like I need a girlfriend. – 1   _____

Uncomfortable. – 3

I'm content without one. – 5

QUESTION

As you walk to your car, a lady in front of you drops a grocery bag, and articles scatter. What do you do?

ANSWER   SCORE

Laugh out loud and point. – 1   _____

Determine to invent better bags. – 3

Help her pick them up. – 5

QUESTION

While you are with your girlfriend, the kissing goes on too long, and she wants you to have sex with her. You've pledged to be abstinent. What would you do?

Do the horizontal mambo. – 1   ____

Compromise and only do some things to make her happy. – 3

Tell her that I respect her too much to take advantage of her (then do 100 push-ups followed by a cold shower!). – 5

QUESTION

Have you ever flirted with another girl when you're dating someone else?

ANSWER   SCORE

Of course. Who hasn't? – 1   ____

Only a couple of times. – 3

Never—that's wrong. – 5

QUESTION

When you walk across the gym floor during a game, what do you think most about?

ANSWER   SCORE

How strong I look. – 1   ____

If people think I look cool. – 3

What flavor of popcorn to buy. – 5

QUESTION

When you're meeting a girl's parents, what's the first thing you do?

ANSWER   SCORE

Mumble a greeting and get out of there ASAP. – 1   ____

Say hi, then see what they're cooking for dinner. – 3

Shake the father's hand, look him in the eye, and get to know him. – 5

How many times a day do you brush your teeth?

SCORE

Brush my what? – 1   ____
Once or twice. – 3
Three times or more. – 5

How often do you shower and use deodorant?

SCORE

Once a week. (Hey, love me for me!) – 1   ____
Every other day. – 3
At least once a day, depending on sports and other
activities. – 5

Do you complete your responsibilities daily?

SCORE
No. – 1   ____
Sometimes. – 3
Yes. – 5

If you are on a diet and someone offers you dessert that is way
beyond the diet's rules, what would you do?

SCORE
Eat it. I'm not hung up about rules. – 1   ____
Only take a bite or eat a small portion. – 3
Kindly refuse. I'm strict on myself. – 5

                                                      _____

                                              TOTAL SCORE

26–61 Dude, you may be a *great* guy. But it'll help your relationships immensely if you work harder on your inner qualities and strengths. One good way is to contact a youth worker or adult to mentor you.

62–96 You're on your way! Work harder on the character development aspects of your life. Study the fruit of the Spirit (see Galatians 5:22-23) for a great way to challenge yourself. Making yourself more attractive on the inside may cause more social interest.

97–130 You rock! You're a great catch, no doubt. Revisit the lower test scores above and see if they indicate how to help better yourself even more!

What did you discover? I hope you're happy with the results. It's just a way to see how you rate in areas of hygiene, character, lifestyle, and future plans.

Be the Right One

Those quizzes bring up a valuable truth. Becoming your best you is essential for finding the right husband or wife. Might sound strange, but would *you* date *you*? Are you preparing yourself to be the ideal your ideal is looking for?

A simple equation: $\frac{1}{2} + \frac{1}{2} \neq$ whole. In other words, you can't be a half person, meet another half person, and expect to make a whole, happy couple. You have to be a whole person first, content with yourself and knowing where you're going in life.

$$\frac{1}{2} + \frac{1}{2} \neq \text{whole.}$$

In an earlier chapter we discussed reconnecting with yourself and discovering what your purpose is. If you don't know who you are and where you're going in life, you're not ready to join your life with someone else's. And that someone else will need to know those answers too, or he or she will just ride along on your plans until things begin to disintegrate.

Here are a few basic guidelines to follow while you're dating. If you date well, you will develop good habits to take with you into your marriage someday.

1. Make sure you have a right relationship with Christ.
2. Know who you are.
3. Set standards and stick to them.
4. Plan your dates carefully.
5. Hold yourself accountable.
6. Remember you don't have to *do* anything sexually to be loved.

God loves relationships, and he wants you to have fantastic ones of your own. But make sure you're ready first.

Choose the Right One

One lady told me that her mother always said to her when she was a teen, "If you can't imagine yourself growing old with this guy, sitting in a rocker and holding his hand, then he isn't for you. And if you can't imagine yourself throwing up from the flu and having this guy hold your head while you do, this guy isn't for you either. Good looks go out the window as you age; quality and loyalty don't."

Headed in the Same Direction

I know many couples who got married just after college and are now getting divorced. Here's one example shared by a friend: A guy was convinced he was going to be a doctor, so his girlfriend married him, all excited that he was going to med school. Four years and two kids later, this guy decided he wanted to run a football camp for boys. Very different salary than his wife had envisioned. They wound up divorcing. Their story shows how important a solid foundation is in the first place. If you're going to get married, you have time. A person who really loves you won't walk away if you say you want to be careful and take your time in the relationship. After all, if you marry this person, you'll have the rest of your lives together!

Too many young adults marry too quickly, before they've seen the "real" other person. The big "surprise" after marriage should be the wonder of sex, not how the other person responds to life.

On the road to finding love, how can you de-

> The big "surprise" after marriage should be the wonder of sex, not how the other person responds to life.

velop a long-lasting, fulfilling relationship? One that will have a high level of intimacy (a soul-to-soul connection) and romance—but none of the strings, pressures, and regrets of sex outside of marriage? One that limits disappointments?

It all starts with realizing the difference between expectations and hopes.

Expectations ... or Hopes?

When you think about someone to date, what are you expecting to find? Maybe "Wow—I just know she'll have the perfect body" or "He'll be the guy every girl wants to date"?

Let's talk straight here. If you expect to have the *perfect* date, most likely you'll be disappointed. No one is perfect. Having a huge list of expectations sets you up for a fall.

But hopes—now, those are different. You can always set your hopes high. For example, you can hope for a guy who's romantic and brings you flowers or a girl who shares your love of sports. But realize you probably won't find someone who meets all your hopes. Instead, you'll discover someone with qualities you may not even know you want.

Keep in mind the difference between expectations and hopes. Your expectations should be your list of "nonnegotiables." Here's 17-year-old Kara's list.

Kara's Nonnegotiables

The person I date must:
- Not only be a Christian, but a growing Christian, interested in spiritual things.
- Be a gentleman (open doors for me).
- Not push for sexual favors or even a kiss on a date, just because we went out.
- Respect me—and my opinion—and not just assume that since I'm a girl, I'm dumb.

What are *your* nonnegotiables? Why not write them down on paper now, so you won't be swayed when somebody who's especially hot or intriguing comes along?

And what about your hopes? Here's Kara's list of hopes.

Kara's Hopes

The person I date will hopefully:
- Like playing tennis, just like me.
- Be dark-haired, handsome, and tall.
- Play the piano and sing me romantic songs by candlelight.
- Be considered cool by my friends.
- Be in the same year in school as me and in a lot of my classes.

When you find yourself "shopping" for the right one, be very aware of the complicated issues that make up a relationship. You don't have to commit to a "purchase" yet. Just enjoy meeting people.

If you ask God for guidance and take your time, he will guide you. So pace yourself and enjoy life for now!

12

lead the way
Choose

Now is the time.

Long ago a great biblical war hero named Joshua had a choice to make. He chose to challenge his nation. "Choose today whom you will serve. . . . But as for me and my family, we will serve the Lord." Even after Joshua, as leader, had laid out the challenge, the people *still* had to make a choice. They knew their history and had seen the power of their God. They also had seen the juicy seduction offered by the other gods and lifestyles. What would they choose? Could they sit quietly and simply not commit?

Choosing not to act is still a choice.

I personally don't think it's possible. You see, even choosing not to act is still a choice.

Now that you have the information, you are responsible. And you are either on one side or the other.

Where do you stand? The line is drawn. When it comes to your beliefs and habits about sex, are you on God's team or your own? If you're on your own team, then you'll eventually end up on Twisted's.

You can make changes happen. But change will come only as you move forward.

> **Change will come only as you move forward.**

You are not alone.

Living on God's team won't always be easy. But you are not alone. You've read personal notes from other teens who are choosing to do things God's way. Here are a few more:

Two years ago I made a promise to God that I wouldn't kiss a guy until I was 16. It's been so hard, but I will always be true to God.

—Loren, TX

When we were first told about this assembly my friends and I thought we were going to listen to some fat guy who never did anything but talk. (I just had to share that with you!) You've made me, a virgin, more aware of what is out there. As a Christian, I hope and pray that everyone in my school got the same messages that I got. One thing my boyfriend commented about was how right you were. He's a virgin too. Both of us agreed to your statement about sex in high school before marriage ruining relationships. Some of our friends who had been together for only a few months did it and broke up within a few days.

—Janice, NY

It's great to realize that I'm not stupid and ridiculous for feeling the way I feel. I'm waiting until marriage to have sex. I see too many girls wandering around pregnant and it's very sad.

—Faith, OK

I'm a new Christian who is committed to staying abstinent, to living up to my goals, and to hopefully persuading others through my actions that they can also respect their bodies by not giving in to the pressures that we face every day. We are constantly told through advertising and other propaganda that we "have" to do certain things because everyone does it and we are expected to—it's normal to have sex and do drugs and party with our friends as teenagers in today's world. I have had to sit through so many school presentations where, instead of promoting abstinence, they just show us how to use condoms or other forms of birth control. It's like they're telling us "we know you are going to do it because that's what we expect from you so here's what you can do (in your words) to 'make it safer.'" Doug, you made a lot of girls really proud of their decisions to stay virgins, and you made a lot of kids rethink where their lives are headed.

—Kortney, FL

I made a decision a long time ago to remain pure until I get married. But you see, a lot of times this year people have tried to get me to give it up. But still I have stayed pure. As a matter of fact, one of those guys was in the audience today! Take that—I hope he felt guilty!

—Jennifer, CA

Before I had reasons to wait. Now I'm full of reasons to wait.

—Dayna, PA

I am thankful that I have kept my virginity. All my friends have lost theirs and they all talk about it. Up until [your presentation] today I'd felt weird that I still have mine. Thank you.

—Taryn, NY

So many people your age are still virgins. And for those of you who are not, you have the chance to start over. Renew your commitment to come clean. All you have to do is ask God to cleanse your life, clear your mind, and forgive you of your past. Then make a very real commitment to start over. Write it as a letter to yourself if you need to. Place that letter in a sealed envelope and put it somewhere as a reminder to yourself. That blank page is waiting for your story. Don't let someone else push the pen across the paper for you. Begin writing to your future spouse and share your desire to start over today. You are a *renewed* virgin!

Yeah, everyone has a past. But Someone changed all that long ago.

Jesus began a revolution, and he is inviting you to be like him. You have the opportunity to lead the way for your friends.

A Line in the Sand

The crowd surrounds you as you square off. A line has been drawn in the sand before you. You have been challenged by someone who disagrees with what you believe and what you stand for.

"Fight!" some stranger yells.

All eyes focus on you. Do you cross the line or not? If you walk away, they will label you a coward or say you don't care. If you stay, you'll be in the thick of the battle.

Your heart is racing, and your hands turn clammy and cold. When you look around, all you can see are the faces of people who've stopped to see what your decision will be. They chant in unison, *"Fight. Fight. Fight. Fight."*

A gap in the crowd opens and you see someone farther off, kneeling. His dark, flowing hair and neat beard remind you of a man you heard of years before. It's Jesus. He holds a simple stick in his hand, and he is writing in the sand. You can't totally make out everything it says, but the words *life, respect,* and *clean* are legible.

The crowd presses closer, continuing their crazed chant. This man underlines a word and turns to look at you. His eyes pour into your soul a marvelous sense of power and purpose. Encouragement floods your heart. He winks, turns back to his lines in the sand, and the crowd blocks your view of him.

Then you start to grin as you realize that Christ too had to cross a line once—a line that separated us from the Creator. Because he crossed that line, he provided true freedom and renewed cleanliness for each of us. In the flash of an eye, it becomes clear to you what you must do.

In your mind you can see the faces of millions of your peers. All are looking to you, calling for help, as Twisted strikes at their innocence, ripping away at their purity. He growls and glares over his shoulder at you, his eyes narrowing in anger.

Then a whisper moves and grows within you. You know it's Jesus, speaking directly to your soul: *I've given you my blood, my name, my Word, and my Spirit. I will never leave you.*

A line is drawn. The crowd awaits. What will you do?

Want to know what other teens are asking?

You've heard from a lot of teens in this book already. Here are some more straight-up e-mail questions and my answers.

How far can I go?

Q: How far is too far?

A: This is a question you and your parents need to decide—before going out on a date. But you know what? Every week I meet teens who haven't set any boundaries for appropriate behavior, so they allow themselves to be led further than they want to go, due to the passion of the moment. And every week I meet thousands of teens whose parents have not given them any direction, so the teens are deciding the answer to this question on their own.

But for now, in addressing this answer, we must first address the *question*. The question you really want to ask is, "How far can I go?"

But let me ask *you* a question—"How far can you go until *what*?" What do you think "too far" is? Is it pregnancy? Then vaginal intercourse without *guaranteed* contraception is out, if that is your only concern. But what about STDs? Then *any* genital contact of any kind should be avoided. If your concern is date rape or uncontrolled sexual arousal, then prolonged kissing and caressing are out.

Do you see where I'm headed with this? I'll be blunt: *The line you should never cross is the tan line.* Yes, that's right, don't cross the tan line. Because if the sun doesn't touch it, *nobody else's son better touch it either!*

My friend is pregnant.

Q: My friend who is 16 is pregnant. I feel that I should support her in her decisions, but I also know that what she did was wrong. What should I do?

A: This is a great question! I've seen churches parade a pregnant teen girl before the congregation and make her confess her sins. That's uncalled for and humiliating.

Sin is sin, period. We can't escape the reality of that. But everything I say here is interwoven with compassion. So what should you do?

1. Be a friend first. Before you can talk about important issues, you have to have her trust and respect.
2. Help her (and the father) realize that sex outside of marriage is wrong. There's no exception. And because it's spiritually wrong, there's a consequence for it. Research shows on average that this young child will not fare as well as children raised in a committed marriage by a mother and a father.
3. Offer hope and life. Affirm her decision not to have an abortion. While the baby was conceived in sin, the baby is a gift of God, not a "mistake." You see, God specializes in grace. This is a good example of it.
4. That said, encourage her to see how aborting is eliminating life. Abortion never removes the "problem." Placing the child for adoption takes great courage and compassion, but it is done every day. Encourage her to think about what is best for the baby, not just for herself.

There is no pat answer for this question. Instead, move slowly in your relationship with your friend, and process each of these consequences and factors as they come up. If someone misreads your love and compassion for her as acceptance of teen pregnancy, then he or she may be too shallow to understand the truth. So don't hold back compassion to someone based on what you think others may think. Love her as Christ loved the woman caught in adultery. He defended her, forgave her, addressed her sin, and challenged her to stop sinning (see John 8:1-11).

Speed Dating?

Q: What is speed dating?

A: The term traditionally has been used to define an evening of mini-dates among single adults. Equal numbers of men and women meet at a predetermined place and talk with members of the opposite sex for three to eight minutes each. If they want to get to know a person better, they make a note on a chart given to them at the beginning of the evening. As each period of time is up, they move to the next person in line for another mini-date.

However, among the 13–18 crowd, speed dating now refers to quick sex with a member of the opposite gender. It's the same concept as a one-night stand, only it happens in five to ten minutes, in a place like a bathroom or a car.

What if she doesn't want to change?

Q: I have a really good friend who has gone too far with guys who later gave her a bad reputation because of it. But she's proud of what she did. How can I help my friend stop doing this and not get into trouble?

A: How can you change a friend's behavior when she doesn't want to change? You can't. Obviously, you can pray for her. But maybe it will help if you spend more time connecting with her, heart-to-heart. As you get even closer, find out what her dreams, goals, and hopes are in life. These "soft spots" in her soul will help you figure out what's most important to her. I believe you can find a way to show her why she should stop damaging her mind, body, and relationships. Show her that God offers more for her, beginning with a new start.

My friend is gay.

Q: How do I give this information on abstinence and purity to my gay friends?

A: Here's a letter from Michelle, a teen girl in New York, that may help:

> I'm a junior and am 16 years old. I'm the only person at our school who is known as being gay. I've been "out" for three years, and though it has gotten easier to walk the halls, it is still very hard. Through your speech you said that to love, it does not matter what you look like but who you are within. Many people only see me as a lesbian and don't realize that there is more to me which I am hoping they will now understand since they heard your speech. I'm not saying that your message on abstinence didn't hit home with me, but also the deeper message is what truly moved me. You've changed the way I look at life, and I hope that you also helped other kids within our school.

To reach our gay and lesbian friends, we must lead with our heart, talk about true love, and encourage sexual and emotional health through abstinence until marriage. No judgment allowed. Our compassionate attitude, words, and actions may show them God's plan for sex and marriage and release them from Twisted's snare.

A Messed-Up Friend

Q: I have a friend who has older guys messing with her. The last guy she was with was seven years older than her. She's starting to take drugs and that's definitely not good for her health. What do I do? Her family is really, really messed up, and her mom doesn't seem to care what happens as long as she has a pack of cigarettes. How can I help my friend?

A: Ouch. That's an example of one of the hundreds of teens I meet every week in schools. First, build a relationship with her and establish trust and respect. Then you can talk with her about her relationships. I'm sure she's craving the love and acceptance of an older man, which is common for those who don't have that from a father figure. When we try to meet our emotional needs with sex, we get into trouble. Find out what she cares about, and see if she can change her behavior to fight for her own sense of worth and value. Also, if she can find a good church that can help her see that God wants to be her heavenly Father who can satisfy her heart, she can work on a relationship with him that will fulfill her desire for belonging that she's looking for from this older guy. Not only that, but through Christ and the Holy Spirit, God can also fulfill her desire to be valued and to have purpose.

Does it hurt?

Q: Hey man, I am a virgin and some of my friends say it hurts really bad to lose your virginity. That's one of the reasons I'm staying a virgin. Is that true?

A: If you are a guy, it typically doesn't hurt that bad. If you are a girl, it depends on several factors, like whether your hymen is intact or not and the amount of natural or applied lubricant. Yes, it can hurt, but it's best to get the accurate medical information about this from your doctor (gynecologist for you girls). If you are in a marriage, then you have years to practice having sex. Years! *Hundreds* of sexual experiences. So when the bride and groom take their time, it isn't that bad. Unmarried teens and young adults are usually overly excited, and the nervous, clumsy actions can make it painful. Bottom line? Wait till you're married and have your spouse take his or her time.

How do I know what I like?

Q: How do I find out what I like in a guy so I will know what I'm looking for?

A: This applies to guys and girls both. You can't know what you like in the opposite sex if you're never around them, right? So spend time with them. *But* do it in safe and varied situations. Watch couples with good marriages and see how they treat each other. If the guy is just with guys, does he act differently or say different things about his wife than when he's with her? Compare what you learn from these men and women with the teens you know. Look for key character traits that you value.

Physically, your body is changing even as you read this. It will continue to change throughout the rest of your life. So find someone whose body is only a secondary accent to the beauty of his or her inner character. That person is a keeper! The body will change, so don't let it worry you.

Also, make sure you're learning from God's Word. Look at it this way: Bank tellers spend a lot of time with real money. A fake is easy to spot because it sticks out. Spending time with God in his Word helps you experience what is real when it comes to character and the spirit. Then when you bump into someone who is fake inside, you'll know.

Only One Person?

Q: Is there a perfect match for me? Only one person?

A: Maybe you're wondering, *What if there is one person God has planned for me and something happens so we don't connect? If God has only one person for me, my soul mate, can I mess this up and miss that person?*

Perhaps it's because I've been married twice, but I personally don't think God is that trivial. I don't believe God has "just one person" for you. I believe that if you're asking God to help you choose wisely, then the person you choose to marry is the one God has for you.

A cop-out, you say? I don't think so. The Bible offers foundational truths concerning our daily needs, such as the promise of Matthew 6:33: "He will give you all you need from day to day if you live for him and make the Kingdom of God your primary concern." And Psalm 37:4: "Take delight in the Lord, and he will give you your heart's desires." That means that as long as your heart is God's and your mind has his priorities, your decisions will be right.

But how will you know which decision is correct when there is more than one person to choose from? or which date is a potential spouse? Great questions. Many times when I was dating I found God saying no to me. It wasn't like a voice speaking out loud, but rather a gentle conviction in my gut. *No, Doug. Nope, not her. Not her either. Her? No way. Nope.* The no's usually came because I knew that there were foundational issues we didn't agree on. I also found God saying, *Okay. Okay. Okay.* Sometimes he lets you choose. And then if you allow yourself to be guided by prayer, supported by a lot of godly counsel, and you make the choice based on faith, that choice is the right one. For me, it was that way with Evon. Then two years after Evon's death, it was that way with Stephanie.

If you have physical or medical questions, please talk to your physician.

To read other straight-up questions or to ask one of your own, go to **PureRevolution.com.** I'd love to hear from you!

Chapter 1

p. 2 (his third law of motion) "Newton's Laws of Motion," *The Physics Classroom* (December 30, 2002), http://www.glenbrook.k12.il.us/gbssci/phys/Class/newtlaws/u2l4a.html.

p. 3 (I'll call Kari) Names have been changed throughout the book unless someone granted permission to use his or her name.

Chapter 3

p. 17 ("Really?" he asked) Genesis 3:1-7

p. 19 (Accepting this gift) Adapted from a paper, "General Audience: The Nuptial Meaning of the Body" (dated January 9, 1980), given to me by a dear friend in Edmonton, Alberta, Canada.

p. 19 ("I am the way") John 14:6

p. 19 ("I am the resurrection") John 11:25

Chapter 4

p. 22 ("parent connectedness") Adapted from Robert W. Blum, M.D., quoted in Anita M. Smith, ed., *Protecting Adolescents from Risk: Transcript of a Capitol Hill Briefing on New Finding from the National Longitudinal Study of Adolescent Health* (Washington, D.C.: Institute for Youth Development, 1999), 43–44.

p. 28 (God wants you) 1 Thessalonians 4:3-7

p. 28 ("For God has not") 2 Timothy 1:7

Chapter 6

p. 46 (As a result) Bridget Maher, ed., *The Family Portrait: A Compilation of Data, Research and Public Opinion on the Family* (Washington, D.C.: Family Research Council, 2002), 165–166.

p. 47 (The reality is) Rebecca A. Maynard, *Kids Having Kids: Economic and Social Consequences of Teen Pregnancy* (Washington, D.C.: Urban Institute Press, 1996), 2–5.

p. 47 (Most are still) Maher, *The Family Portrait,* 165–166.

p. 47 (Studies show) Ibid., 165–166.

p. 47 ("Here is how") John 15:13

p. 48 (the Bible says) See Jeremiah 1:4-5 and Psalm 139:13.

p. 48 (Roughly 3,000 abortions) "Surveillance Summaries," *Morbidity and Mortality Weekly Report* 49, no. 11 (December 8, 2000): 1–44, http://www.cdc.gov/mmwr/preview/mmwrhtml/ss4911a1.htm.

p. 48 ("You watched me") Psalm 139:15-16

p. 48 (In the United States) M. Freundlich, "Supply and Demand: The Forces Shaping the Future of Infant Adoption," *Adoption Quarterly* 2, no. 1 (1998): 13–42.

p. 50 (Sadly, less than) K. A. Moore et al., *Beginning Too Soon: Adolescent Sexual Behavior, Pregnancy, and Parenthood* (Washington, D.C.: ChildTrends, 1995).

p. 50 ("Sweetheart, I'm leaving") Thanks to Wade Horn from the U.S. Department of Health and Human Services, who shared this hypothetical story at a Strengthening Families Conference in Denver, Colorado, September 18, 2002.

p. 51 (*Love* can mean") American Social Health Association, "Sex on the Brain" (May 28, 2002), www.iwannaknow.org/brain2/index.html.

p. 53 (fruits of the Spirit) See Galatians 5:22-23.

Chapter 7

p. 56 (Each year) "It's Your (Sex) Life: Your Guide to Safe and Responsible Sex" (Henry J. Kaiser Family Foundation and MTV, 2002), 12.

p. 56 (And two-thirds) T. R. Eng and W. T. Butler, eds., *The Hidden Epidemic—Confronting Sexually Transmitted Disease* (Washington, D.C.: National Academy Press, 1997).

p. 56 (Doctors believe) "STDs: The Facts," a brochure (Austin, Tex.: The Medical Institute, 2001), 2.

p. 56 (More sexual partners) Eng and Butler, *The Hidden Epidemic.*

p. 56 (So what are) In order to lessen confusion, I've used STD throughout this book.

p. 56 (They can be put into) There is also a third category of parasites, called protozoal.

p. 56 (Bacterial infections) Deborah D. Cole and Maureen Gallagher Duran, *Sex and Character* (Richardson, Tex.: Foundation for Thought and Ethics, 1998), 71–73.

p. 57 (But treatments) "STDs: The Facts," 2.

p. 57 (Worse, young women) Centers for Disease Control and Prevention (CDC), "Tracking the Hidden Epidemics: Trends in STDs in the United States 2000," 4, http://www.cdc.gov/nchstp/dstd/Stats_Trends/Trends2000.pdf.

p. 57 (Let's start with) For more information on other STDs, see Doug Herman,

Time for a Pure Revolution, chapter 7, and the resources section at the back of that book.

p. 57 (If untreated) CDC, "Tracking the Hidden Epidemics," 6.

p. 57 (Both men and women) Cole and Duran, *Sex and Character*, 72.

p. 57 (Infected people) CDC, "Tracking the Hidden Epidemics," 9.

p. 57 (Unborn and newborn babies) Cole and Duran, *Sex and Character,* 72.

p. 59 (HSV outbreaks) Ibid., 80.

p. 59 (Herpes is for life) Ibid.

p. 59 (More than one in five) CDC, "Tracking the Hidden Epidemics," 2.

p. 59 (But "with or without") Ibid., 20.

p. 60 (Roughly 120,000) Ibid., 22.

p. 61 (There are an estimated) See the Web site www.cdc.gov/nchstp/od/news/At-a-Glance.pdf.

p. 61 (Three years ago) Centers for Disease Control and Prevention, "U.S. HIV and AIDS Cases Reported through December 2001," *HIV/AIDS Surveillance Report* 13, no. 2, http://www.cdc.gov/hiv/stats/hasr1302.htm.

p. 62 (That makes it) CDC, "Tracking the Hidden Epidemics," 2.

p. 62 (Over 30 of these) American Social Health Association (ASHA), "HPV: Get the Facts," http://www.ashastd.org/hpvccrc/quickfaq.html.

p. 62 (The HPV virus) J. Walboomers et al., "Human Papillomavirus Is a Necessary Cause of Invasive Cancer Worldwide," *Journal of Pathology* 189 (1999): 12–19; K. L. Wallin et al., "Type-Specific Persistence of Human Papillomavirus DNA Before the Development of Invasive Cervical Cancer," *New England Journal of Medicine* 341, no. 22 (1999).

p. 62 (That makes HPV) ASHA, "HPV: Get the Facts"; L. A. G. Ries et al., eds., "SEER Cancer Statistics Review, 1973–1996" (Bethesda, Md.: National Cancer Institute, 1999); "Trends in Sexual Risk Behaviors among High School Students—United States, 1991–1997," *Morbidity and Mortality Weekly Report* 47 (1998): 749–752; Centers for Disease Control and Prevention, "U.S. HIV and AIDS Cases Reported through December 2001," *HIV/AIDS Surveillance Report* 13, no. 2, http://www.cdc.gov/hiv/stats/hasr1302.htm.

p. 63 (And the list) Cole and Duran, *Sex and Character,* 84.

p. 64 (Take this self-test) Statistics are taken from the "Contraceptive Protection Rate Chart" in Marilyn Morris, *Choices That Lead to Lifelong Success* (Dallas, Tex.: Charles River Publishing Company, 1998), 158. Morris's original source for this data was Rita Rubin, "News You Can Use—Birth Control Failure," data from The Alan Guttmacher Institute, *U.S. News and World Report,* 3 March 1997, 67.

Chapter 8
p. 77 (sexual harassment) For a specific definition of sexual harassment, go to http://www.sexualharassmentpolicy.com/default.htm.

Chapter 9
p. 85 ("I say, anyone") Matthew 5:28

p. 88 (Masturbation is) For more information, see Doug Herman, *Time for a Pure Revolution* (Wheaton, Ill.: Tyndale House Publishers, 2004), chapter 1, under the heading "Common Hot Questions."

p. 89 ("Fix your thoughts") Philippians 4:8

Chapter 10
p. 91 (She spends her time) Visit www.ibreakdown.com for a very exciting Web site!

p. 94 (A woman is only) Marilyn Morris, *Choices That Lead to Lifelong Success* (Dallas, Tex.: Charles River Publishing Company, 1998), 30–33.

Chapter 12
p. 115 ("Choose today") Joshua 24:15

Heart-gripping... Breathtaking... He made us laugh and cry at the same time!

That's what you'll hear from students and adults who have listened to Doug Herman share his passion. His zany humor blends with his tragic story to make a life-changing impact. Listening to him animate scripture (How *did* they get that paralyzed guy through the ceiling?) is "spiritual edu-tainment."

In the five churches where Doug has served, ranging in size from 250 to 7,000 members, he has pastored four youth groups. That means he has experienced scores of eye-blurring lock-ins, unending hours at youth camps in the mountains and on beaches, and youth retreats that have scarred him (literally). He's had so many wild youth events occur that he's listed in *Group*'s *All Star Bloopers!* He's also been a high school wrestling coach and a substitute teacher. Now Doug is an international speaker and author, with over 20 years in youth and family ministry.

While a youth pastor, Doug lost his wife and infant daughter to AIDS through infected blood in a transfusion. Yes, he was shaken. But he emerged from this tragedy passionate about the message of purity, respect, and honor. He wanted to offer students, families, and communities a Pure Revolution—life rather than death. It was a vow he made at his daughter's deathbed.

Thirteen years and over 2,000 school assemblies later, the Pure Revolution Project was born, and it's been growing ever since through high school assembly programs and Pure Revolution Conferences he conducts nationally each year. He also loves speaking at churches, youth conferences, and festivals, bringing fresh passion to dry hearts and courageous motivation to the masses.

Currently, Doug speaks over 100 days a year, giving 300 presentations annually to teens—and the adults who love them—about character development, sexual abstinence, and spiritual passion. He's been interviewed on over 200 national radio and television programs in addition to his new radio program, *Pure Revolution Radio.* His first two books, *What Good Is God? Finding*

Faith and Hope in Troubled Times (Baker, 2002) and *FaithQuake: Rebuilding Your Faith after Tragedy Strikes* (Baker, 2003), have received great reviews from a broad-based readership. He has published articles in *Youthworker*, *Living with Teenagers*, *ParentLife*, and *Leadership Journal*.

Now remarried to Stephanie, Doug enjoys balancing scuba diving, golf, and salsa dancing with his activities as father to Josh (like watching him compete in paintball tournaments), Bri (like playing any type of game with her . . . and losing), and Luc (like watching "guy movies" with popcorn and their shirts off)!

To launch your own Pure Revolution event for your community, or to schedule Doug for your next event or school assembly, *simply visit our Web site and get a clean start!*

PureRevolution.com

Okay, you know

your parents want

to know what your

life is like . . .

. . . maybe they think the pressures you face every day are the same as when they were in high school.

Here's a way to tell them the truth—to let them know what you're up against from the moment you wake up. They can pick up the book by Doug Herman written to parents called *Time for a Pure Revolution*.

ISBN 0-8423-8357-3
Price $13.99

check out

purerevolution.com

areUthirsty.com

well . . . are you?

degrees OF guilt

Sammy's dead...they each played a part.
Kyra, his twin sister. Miranda, the girl he
loved. And Tyrone, a friend from school.

WHAT'S THE REAL STORY?

There's always more than
one point of view—read all three.

kyra's story
{DANDI DALEY MACKALL}

ISBN 0-8423-8284-4

miranda's story
{MELODY CARLSON}

ISBN 0-8423-8283-6

tyrone's story
{SIGMUND BROUWER}

ISBN 0-8423-8285-2

degreesofguilt.com

ANOTHER TITLE FROM

Jennifer Knapp

ZOEgirl

Ginny Owens

Stacie Orrico

Superchic[k]

Jaci Velasquez

Rebecca St. James

Ever worry about where your life is going?

Some of the most popular singers in Christian music face the same types of struggles you face—loneliness, materialism, feeling ugly, difficult friendships, body image, popularity, and more. Here some of your favorite musicians share their stories and what they've learned from God in the process.

Open the book and step out with friends for a deeper, more intimate relationship with God.

You can't begin a journey without taking a step . . .

areUthirsty.com
ISBN 0-8423-6069-7

best friends
an ocean apart ...
surviving life together

Hands across the
MOON

jane g. meyer

*If you ever need a
shoulder to cry on or
a hand to hold, mine
can reach all the way
across the world.*

Life isn't what best friends Gretchen and Mia had in
mind. They'd looked forward to their junior year together—
in California. Then Gretchen had to move to Ecuador . . . a
world away. Now, nothing's going right for either of them.

*Sometimes it seems that their "across the moon"
letters are their best lifeline.*

areUthirsty.com
ISBN 0-8423-8286-0